The Secret Life
of Husbands

Everything You Need to Know
about the Man in Your Life

MELISSA KATSOULIS

CONSTABLE

CONSTABLE

First published in Great Britain in 2019 by Constable

1 3 5 7 9 10 8 6 4 2

A CIP catalogue record for this book
is available from the British Library.

ISBN: 978-1-47212-993-2

Typeset in Sabon by Hewer Text UK Ltd, Edinburgh
Printed and bound in Great Britain by CPI Group (UK) Ltd, Croydon CR0 4YY

Papers used by Constable are from well-managed
forests and other responsible sources.

Constable
An imprint of
Little, Brown Book Group
Carmelite House
50 Victoria Embankment
London EC4Y 0DZ

An Hachette UK Company
www.hachette.co.uk

www.littlebrown.co.uk

THE SECRET LIFE
OF HUSBANDS

Contents

Foreword

What do our husbands talk about with their friends? What do they do when they're home alone? Do they really not know how to do laundry? Do they hate our mothers?

I'm longing to find out. With masculinity in crisis (again), it's more important than ever to understand the secret lives of husbands. If the gender power-imbalance is to be better understood and readjusted, we're going to have to look, as impartially as possible and with as much good humour as we can muster, at how the world looks from inside a man's head. Is his life's journey from son to husband traumatic? Is he just a walking Venn diagram of sport and self-abuse? I don't believe that. I don't think . . .

But their mysterious ways perplex me. Those guys on *Grand Designs* who make their wives and babies huddle in damp caravans for two years while they doggedly perfect some huge, bankrupting edifice to masculine folly; the husband of a friend who, discovering the rental car's speakers were broken on their honeymoon, proceeded to pop on his headphones and listen to their chosen driving music on his own; all those famous men who have sex in cupboards and text pictures of their willies. What are they thinking?

I've been hunting husbands since I was a child. Growing up without a dad, I was intrigued by families with a man about the house, and watched like a miniature anthropologist for what these big, hairy creatures got up to. Some watched telly and smoked. Others worked upstairs in their studies on mysterious projects. Some shouted, cried or even danced around the kitchen table in tiny denim shorts.

Hanging out at the Greenham Common peace camp with my mother in the 1980s made husbands seem even more exotic, since even the softest of spouses could only be there with express permission from a female gatekeeper.

When I became a teenager, my doomed search for the perfect boyfriend was supplemented by feverish background reading on what made men tick, and why relationships succeed or fail. The letters and diaries of heroes and reprobates from Byron to Dickens and Sackville-West left me none the wiser about marriage but gave me a hunger to understand the aliens in our midst. By then, I had access to warts 'n' all relationship chat from the woman's side (my mother's friends, magazines and of course novels) but I wanted more.

Finally, as an adult, and a happily married one (maybe all that juvenile research did help me close in on a prime specimen), a couple of eye-opening events made me think more seriously about the nature of the modern husband.

One was reading Karl Ove Knausgård's *My Struggle*, the longest insider account of husband-ing ever written; and the other was a chance conversation with my own husband. He had overheard me chatting to a girlfriend. Just the usual banter: faux-desperate accounts of our sex lives post-kids; the sad, empty crisp packets where our gorgeous boobs used to be; how no one will ever again be rendered helpless – unless with laughter – by the sight of our naked bodies.

My husband was shocked. How could I share such personal information?

'Come on,' I said, 'don't you talk like that with your mates?'

'Absolutely not!'

'What do you talk about then?'

'You know – politics, schools . . .'

Oh.

Now, some men surely do dish the dirt on their intimate relationships, and with a bit of prodding my husband agreed that, occasionally, sordid tales of stag-night shenanigans are cheerfully shared. But never anything to do with their spouses. That would be disrespectful. A marriage is private and sacred and I, with my low talk, had clearly not recognised that.

I felt genuinely sorry and a bit ashamed but mostly wildly intrigued. What was going on here?

Why do husbands and wives have such different standards? Why do husbands hate to risk oversharing, whereas women's friendships are forged and strengthened precisely by making themselves vulnerable through personal disclosure?

With some men I talked to for this project, there was a simple caveman vibe to their closed-offness: if they went around crying and navel-gazing, they couldn't get on with the important job of being a tough provider who never takes a day off work and is always a 'rock' to his family, could they? Others, like a man in his fifties who had enjoyed the classic English treat of being sent away to boarding school at a young enough age, thus completely stuffing up any emotional responses for decades afterwards, happily said that his spouse has allowed him to become a more open person. 'She has taught me to be the person I always wanted to be, but couldn't,' he said, hinting that he no longer feels it's shameful to show and share his feelings.

So much of what we do each day is motivated by shame, and the role that heterosexual marriage has in how shameful it feels to open yourself up to the world is fascinating to me, and should be for anyone interested in chipping away at the patriarchy. On the face of it, shame is about how others judge you. When you get married (a public vow made in front of your community), you hold yourself up to the judgement of those 'gathered here today' to witness your promise. That's the meaning of a wedding. But after the privileged glimpses into various marriages I've had while researching this book, I think it's our spouses who are the real gatekeepers of our shame. The person you live with every day and who knows you better than anyone and who has the power to make you feel like a mouse or a mensch? That's your partner. Only they know that weird thing you do in the bath, the things that keep you awake at night and the real reason you never see your cousin any more. They are a bit like an arbitrator in a legal dispute: someone you have willingly invited in to judge you. They are also your confidant – the one in front of whom you can cry and who will look after you and hear your whispered fears. So for a husband, a wife becomes not only the manager of his emotional vulnerability but his confessor and comforter too. She offers him a safe place to be himself without being judged, but signals to him when it's time to toughen up as well. Just as his mother once did. She is all he needs, or so he hopes: cue drink, divorce, disgruntlement and general dog-like behaviour when he realises she can't actually fulfil this impossible, mystical role.

Whereas most men are hard to draw out of their shells (especially when you ask questions like 'what do you like to do when your wife goes out?'), some come out all guns blazing with their apparently most shameful secrets: like an ex-boyfriend of mine who I didn't need to interview because he writes publicly with no filter. And I knew about his habits anyway. They haven't changed much since he married his wife (also a good pal of mine): interfering with himself and fretting about fatness are what goes on when he's alone.

It took a psychoanalyst to point out that those who give you their deepest, darkest secrets may be saying, 'Look! Here it all is! There's nothing more for you to see!', using their sordid confessions as a smokescreen for the shameful 1 per cent that they don't want you to find. I know about this because I do it too.

Then there are the really inscrutable fellows, so far along the shame spectrum that they're just one big walking wince. Some, like Karl Ove Knausgård, can only get their dark secrets out by writing them down for millions of strangers to read. I'll never forget the day I got to meet him. We spent an afternoon together on the rain-lashed South Bank of the Thames, chain-smoking (him) and feeling a confusing mixture of adolescent and big-girl emotions (me). This handsome, dark-souled, desperately insecure man spoke, tangentially and in distant whispers, of the impact of being married to a woman with severe mental illness and the joy of raising their beloved children. Love and shame shone with equal intensity from his ice-blue eyes, while he skirted around the fact that he had just left her for a younger model, a fact that I was also too shy to mention. He really hates talking about himself, he admitted. Yet he has achieved global literary stardom by writing it all up in forensic detail, in huge streams of prose that he can't bear to go back and read once it has done its purgative work on him.

My mission in this book is not to find the perfect husband, or the worst. I want to talk to married men and understand their world. How do they feel when their wives scoff at their housekeeping skills, or tell them what to eat? Is the transition from bachelor to husband to father a bit overwhelming? Why do so many widowers swiftly remarry?

There is so much statistical research out there about gender and domestic politics, but it doesn't tell me what I need to know, which is how things really feel to real men. So I'm going to ask them.

And by the way, I'm going to tell you some depressing and dreadful stuff about the good old patriarchy before we get on to laughing at blokes making a mess in the kitchen. Because it's all part of the same complex, beguiling, tragic human soup. So bear with me. Or just skip to the chapter about cooking.

Introduction

Historically, husbands have lived in the shadows. If that sounds a bit sad, think of it as the cool, dappled shade of privilege, which gives you lots of privacy and stops your ice cream from melting. Wives, on the other hand, have always been highly visible objects to be rated, discussed, decorated, denigrated and bargained for. Husbands were the subject of their sentence: their 'husbanding' wasn't really judged because it wasn't even a thing. How to be a certain kind of husband probably didn't occur to a man in England in the sixteenth century when he lay in bed at night thinking over his insecurities, failings and achievements, because his role had the privilege of anonymity. Nothingness, almost. Of course, he wanted power (sexual and commercial) and marriage was the main social structure that let him go after those things. But despite all the fine writing that previous centuries have left us about love, there is little evidence to suggest that 'how to be a husband' was a concept that existed for our funny-hatted forebears. How to be a man, of course, has been discussed ever since cavemen first drew cows on rock. But thinking about the specific role and emotional life of a married man – beyond keeping his wife and feeding his children – is new.

It's happening now because increasingly, all over the world, women have emerged from the objective soup to stand level with men, and this undermines those old, easy identities. In the twenty-first century, many women – but by no means all – have the power to choose or refuse a mate (or choose to have no mate), so their potential life partners have naturally fallen to scrutinising their performance of maleness more closely than ever. What kind of husbanding can they offer?

The women's lib generation thought marriage would be redundant by the twenty-first century, yet wedlock is still a desirable state for most people, such that marriage equality laws have been in the headlines almost constantly for the past ten years. Even those who shrugged off their princess bride fantasies before leaving primary school still want the security and, yes, romance of getting married. Because, after all, love feels good and youthful hope is worth celebrating and no one wants to raise children, die and do all the supermarket shopping alone. Plus weddings seem so important when you've never had one.

There's a problem, though: marriage as a desirable state is the last reliquary of some very old-fashioned ideas about property and power, yet we in the West accept that women are allowed to want traditionally male treats like sexual pleasure, money and interesting jobs. And men are allowed to want a partner who pays half the bills and stands up for herself.

The feminist movements of the past hundred years, while feeling faltering and chaotic to many women, have inflicted a lightning-fast revolution on men, who were resting quite happily on the millennia-old laurels of their good fortune, pipe between teeth and supper regularly on the table, when their womenfolk suddenly seemed to rise up against them.

In the UK, if we take women's suffrage as the beginning of real female emancipation (although the seeds were sown long before, in Mary Wollstonecraft's era), that's a hundred years of revolutionary social upheaval that was twice interrupted by war, which quite naturally drove everyone mad and intensified what could have been a gentler, more considered pace of change. Sending several generations of twentieth-century men off to get slaughtered on the battlefield – and the positive spin everyone had to put on it to get through those devastating days – did deep, dark damage to the reconstructing of male–female relations.

And how much worse for those in mainland Europe, whose lives were deformed by fascism? We often read obituaries, these days, of holocaust survivors. A theme emerges, reading their life stories: many got married very quickly after 1945, often while still in displacement camps. Ad hoc weddings between homeless, traumatised souls showed the power of marriage as symbolic of security and a new start (for the individual and their community, as it would hopefully pave the way for many free and happy babies). It meant normality.*

So: millions of men lost or traumatised; women doing traditionally male work; the mad dreamscape of the upwardly mobile yet repressive 1950s in England and America; the aftershocks of the Industrial Revolution; an increasingly secular society; birth control. All these elements have fed into the unstable ground on which we build our marriages today.

And then there was MeToo. Nowadays, when a man gets into an argument with his wife, he must show his openness to a balanced, respectful exchange of feelings. He must be ready to apologise, acknowledge the crimes of the patriarchy and calmly discuss the disconnect between his and his partner's world-view. He is definitely not supposed to ram his flat cap on his head and storm off to the pub. Because these are good new days. Only, for many men, they don't feel so good. They feel like a time of confusion and upheaval, with no clear instructions on how to 'man' properly. Up? Down? So many options.

Some men regret that they can no longer compliment a lady on looking nice or hold a door open for her without insulting her, yet advertising and social

---

* https://www.nj.com/news/index.ssf/2011/02/nj_holocaust_survivors_share_s.html

media show women as hypersexualised like never before. They know that wolf-whistling is probably wrong, and calling out crude suggestions definitely is, but miss the old-fashioned dance of gent-and-lady that oiled social interaction in the twentieth century and, through the golden age of Hollywood, formed their idea of romance.

Older women, too, have spoken out to say that, in their day, girls had to develop a thick skin and learn to parry the bum-pinchers and patronisers like pre-feminist warriors, and those were actually pretty useful skills to have. When Anne Robinson called the MeToo generation 'wusses' and said that the deplorable behaviour of her male contemporaries only spurred her on to work harder, many ladies of a certain age raised a silent fist-bump to her picture byline.

'Masculinity is in crisis' is a centuries-old concept. Last time it blew up big was at the end of the nineteenth century, when a generation of boys dressed in frilly nighties and raised by females was deemed too girly. So the Boy Scouts movement and laddish adventure stories were invented to get them back out where they belong: in dirty places that spoil your shoes and make you a bit scared. Clearly, Victorian man's concern about his son's gender performance was a reflection of his own anxiety about adult male culture getting a bit out of hand too, with all that flowing hair, flowery fabric and sappy poetry about daffodils and angels. So, fear over the feminisation of men is nothing new, but the buzzwords 'toxic masculinity' and 'MeToo' in our time reflect a new storm in the calm waters of male privilege.

How does this trickle down into the daily life of the modern, married man? I asked some privileged white dudes of my acquaintance and, guess what – they couldn't be more supportive of everything women say about this! We're all totally right (all of us, whatever we think) and yes, it's high time guys did what they were told by us. Can I go now . . . ?

Thanks to my innate female intuition, I think I was able to detect some anxiety here.

So I started out with the basics, asking whether the married guys I know even think of themselves in terms of gender. 'Not at all!' said pretty much the most masculine man I've ever met: a brawny, hairy burgher with a high-status job who prowls around his office all day barking down the phone, then comes home, necks a few beers, strips off his sharp Italian suit and sits in his pants watching sport in between mouthfuls of spicy chicken wings, pausing only to teach his son how to be a kind and honest person, and showing his daughter how to box and shoot hoops. Then he'll fall into a brief, noisy slumber, and wake up with an inspired yet intellectually aggressive new idea about post-Soviet central Asian corporate governance and get straight on Twitter, before diving into a cold lake for a bracing swim before work. And he'll do all this every day, even when he's put his back out, has food poisoning and is caring for two small children all alone. He is literally the manliest man I know. And don't ask me how I know all this about him because my husband does not want to appear in this book. But the point is, he says he never feels aware of being a man, and has no interest in seeking other men to do specifically manly things in a male space. He has even said, in an unguarded moment, that there's no such thing as gender, 'just cool people and dicks'. He has as many female friends as male ones, lesbian and gay mates coming out of his ears, and lifting heavy stuff and drinking six whisky sours without being sick makes him feel no more dudely than wrapping a present really well or sniffing a pretty rose. When I ask him why, he posits that it's all about class and education. He generally doesn't feel threatened by stuff because he was born handsome and healthy to well-off, enlightened parents who sent him to a good school and didn't beat him; so he doesn't have to go out into the world on the defensive. His masculinity doesn't have to be in crisis. Which makes his wife a lucky lady because he probably won't go out and kill himself on a motorbike on his fiftieth birthday.

All this ties in with what the academic Tristan Bridges, a professor of sociology at UCSB, says about the modern gender crisis,[*] namely that for something to be in crisis it has to have been in a period of stasis before, and then one group has to feel things are changing: that their privilege is being undermined.

[*] https://www.aspenideas.org/session/american-man-crisis

Thomas Page McBee, an American writer on gender (and first man of his particular minority to box at Madison Square Gardens), says, 'This crisis, though painful, is also an opportunity to rethink the way gender works ... it's hard work to talk about masculinity because you're not supposed to. It's the first rule – like Fight Club.'* (And he's not the first or last man to invoke the Fight Club analogy when telling me about the golden rule men have of not addressing gender issues.)

Thomas talks about how after transitioning and suddenly looking exactly like a man (he's one of those trans men who pass with ease), he was shocked to find out what male privilege really means in everyday life. In the newsroom where he worked as a journalist, the room now fell silent when he loudly weighed into a spirited group discussion. That had never happened to him before; people had always talked over him. Men on the street kept starting fights with him. Women would be afraid when he walked behind them at night. After his mother died, nobody touched him or comforted him. It's something he believes men should talk about: 'Saying these sorts of things puts you at risk in some ways, professionally and personally ... If men don't say "yes, it's absolutely true", it's gaslighting.'†

There's no doubt that the gender debate is reaching into every corner of our lives, both public and private.

---

* https://www.aspenideas.org/session/american-man-crisis
† Ibid.

So where does this leave the covenant of marriage, an idea rooted in the inequality between men and women? Gay couples have the opportunity to create a new version of it, but a young man and woman wanting to plight their troth these days must take a long, hard look at how to reinterpret the rules to fit twenty-first-century gender roles. For the older generation, it may be too late.

I asked a group of elderly married men whether they thought masculinity was in crisis. They all agreed that 'a certain sort of masculinity is' – the implication being, not their sort. After all, they had kept their wives happy for decades and hadn't been hounded out of their jobs for harassing the tea lady. But there was a discernible reluctance to go further into the outmoded assumptions that underpin their view of gender roles in their family. Who takes the bins out was about as far as they'd go towards confessing they might be a bit old-fashioned. Younger men tended to say 'the hell it is, and quite right too!' in answer to my question, revealing a greater willingness to talk about the shortcomings of their brethren. One, in his late thirties, talked about how standing up to sexism post-MeToo actually made him feel more masculine:

'I feel manly challenging misogyny at work. I mean, when I dare not to bite my tongue and tell that idiot that his jokes about women belonging in the kitchen aren't funny. This is usually followed by a rush of nerves (not so manly) as I know "the pack" will be against me, sometimes including the women. But I know deep down what I've said takes more guts than just going along with the "norm", so I guess that makes me feel proud and manly.'

This radical and fabulous type of behaviour should give hope to us all. But old habits die hard, as Alex, a clinical psychologist, told me when talking about how he senses his own manliness:

'I remember once saying to a (particularly unreconstructed) male flatmate that I had never used a power drill. I can remember his askance look, as if I had confided that I wore women's underwear, and wished him to do so too, perhaps in my presence. This was years ago but clearly it stuck with me. I was doing male incorrectly, but hadn't grasped this until too late. This made me quite furious, though maybe I was trying to regain a sense of masculine agency. I guess what I mean is that I don't particularly seek to feel male, or especially feel it, but I do register when other men notice my doing it wrong, and this has felt humiliating, although I don't feel this is right.

'I probably don't ask for help as much as I should. If I popped in off the street with a full bladder, I wouldn't ask a male barman if I could use the loo. He could say no, and I'd be positioning myself beneath him. It's very weird how male hierarchy gets into you . . .'

I took this issue to *GQ*'s columnist Justin Myers who also writes novels and blogs about contemporary masculinity. I asked him when he feels most manly:

'At the gym. In the locker room – now this is not a thrilling place for me, it reminds me of PE lessons. Not wanting to be there. But as I get older I give less of a fuck, and my most manly time is walking back from shower to my locker. I'm naked, and in that period I feel power I associate with manliness. Not because I have an amazing body but because I don't give a shit.'

It makes sense that realising you don't care about others' criticism makes you feel strong, and Myers links this to the way boys are socialised from an early age: 'It's about independence. Men are taught to seek independence as soon as possible in life – the stabilisers are supposed to come off the bike when you're really young.' Traditionally that has equated to being thick-skinned and tough. When the sociologist Michael Kimmel of Stony Brook University asked a group of marines what qualities they associated with being a good man, they all chorused 'loyalty, decency, honesty, helping the little guy'. The qualities of being a good person, basically. But then he asked them what they associated with 'manning up' and they talked about being tough, suppressing their emotions and not showing pain.

Being a man and behaving manfully are certainly in conflict and probably always have been. Most of the men I asked for insight about what made them feel manly were not sociologists or shrinks or gender bloggers, but just ordinary Joes, sitting in pubs and cafés wearing the uniform of the modern man: smart-casual clothing accessorised with extra pockets, zips, straps and buckles in an oblique reference to all the outdoorsy work with woodpiles they are not doing and the bone-handled awls they're not carrying. Here's what they told me makes them feel like a mensch:

'Providing for and protecting my family.'

'Being good at parking any car. Being unable to forget any number plate.'

'Climbing! Pursuit, wildness, outdoors . . .'

'Lifting things for weaker people.'

'What reminds me most of being male is that we age faster than our wives.'

These responses are exactly what you'd expect men to say, right? But actually enacting – let alone publicly declaring – things like showing your strength at lifting stuff or excellence at parking is likely to make women think you're an unreconstructed he-man. In the old days it didn't matter if a lady thought that about you, because you had all the power. But now it does, because we've started to equalise. So where does the feminist movement leave those qualities that feel like 'core skills' to most men? Neither here nor there, it seems, but waiting at the crossroads, engines revving. On the border between the old ways and whatever comes next. And there's always trouble on the borders . . .

Many of the men I approached asking for a bulletin from the contested territory that is modern marriage simply couldn't do it. Colleagues, academics, politicians, even close friends – people who trust me not to humiliate them – and those who might be said to owe me a favour for, for example, doing the thankless and awkward work of reading and commenting on their cousin's epic, unpublished fantasy novel, ghosted me or just said 'no'. Fellow writers and friends who expose their every marital and sexual secret in the press or at live comedy shows wouldn't talk to me. Yet the insights I did get from those bold enough to get involved with my journey of discovery have been revelatory, and seem to speak much greater truths than statistics.

There won't be many statistics in this book, although I could easily find one to support every mad hypothesis I feel like making. Everyone loves a good hard number with a percentage sign to hold on to, but the real truth about marriage today is not to be found in divorce rates or any of the hundreds of feature-ready bits of sociological research that drop into journalists' in-boxes every week. The truth is in the unexpected things people do.

My love of a good 'dote and its power to tell me the truth about love is what motivated me to write this book and learn what life is like for married men today. How could I not feel blessed and inspired every time someone's husband confided in me that he loves getting stuck into a bit of experimental medicine-making when his wife goes out for the evening? Or that his favourite thing to do is to go to the pub with his newborn baby and eat crisps off its tiny head? Or that he doesn't feel at home in any room in his house because it's not really his domain and he's afraid he might make a mess? This is real life.

There has been so much written about the inner lives of married women. And may my fellow female reporters keep it coming, because we have a great deal of quiet time to make up for. And of course, when we're not writing or reading about the lot of the married lady, we are most likely talking, texting, embroidering, spray-painting or thinking about it. If you're a wife and feeling a bit meh about, say, picking up everyone's socks every day; or if you hate your life; or if no longer fancy your husband; or any number of the infinite silly and serious feelings you might have in any given day, well, as a woman, you know that solidarity, shared experience and a listening ear is only a click away.

But it's different for our husbands. I doubt any married man has waited for his wife to leave the house, then skipped up to his bedroom and gleefully-furiously phoned his best friend and shrieked, 'OMG you will not belieeeeve how long she took in the loo this morning! I had literally unloaded the dishwasher, fed the kids breakfast and concocted a new sexual fantasy about James Franco by the time she had finished crapping.' There are a number of reasons men don't do this: social, ethical, historical and, most of all, emotional. Talking this way makes us vulnerable, which for women is an important way to strengthen our sorority, but for men is unsafe. However, things are changing, and I'm optimistic that the next generation of husbands will create safer, funnier, more easeful ways to share their feelings. I hope that everything I have discovered and recorded in my conversations with ordinary men, experts and imaginary Greek gods will go some way to explaining why this is necessary and what it all means.

Historical Husbands:
Where It All Began

'And the women was sobbin', sobbin', sobbin' passin'
   them nights,
While the Romans was goin' out hobbin', nobbin',
   startin' up fights.'
   from 'Sobbin' Women' by Johnny Mercer, and
   Gene DePaul, *Seven Brides for Seven Brothers*

Marriage has gone through many permutations since the primal sky-deity Uranus mated with his earthy mother-lover Gaia and spawned the twelve titans – shall we take a roll call in case you're looking for baby names? Oceanus, Coeus, Crius, Hyperion, Iapetus, Theia, Rhea, Themis, Mnemosyne, Phoebe, Tethys and Cronus. But the details of their famously rocky marriage (Gaia led their children in rebellion against grumpy Uranus) are lost in the mists of time and anyway would probably be hard for us mortals to relate to.

So it's to the Homeric myths we turn to understand the earliest foundations of Western wedlock. In *The*

Odyssey and *The Iliad* marriage is crucial – Paris and Helen started it all off, ultimately – and it was all about property, power and conflict. Odysseus picked a good long-term prospect in Penelope, but his dalliances with Calypso and Circe gave him a taste of what other versions of love might look like. Circe played the sweet, helpful girl next door, making life so entrancing for him that he didn't want to leave when it was time to move on. Calypso went in harder, trapping him for seven years in the hope of a wedding. She was a great beauty, the daughter of a gangster god (one of Uranus's titans) and beguiled Odysseus with a particularly razzy way she had of swaying about when working her golden loom. You can see why he fell for her. Seven long years she kept him interested, living in sun-drenched bliss on her island, but he missed Penelope so much that finally he left.

What a lot Odysseus had learned about women after all this. Penelope famously didn't recognise him when he first came home to her, and surely it wasn't only age but romantic and sexual wisdom that had made him a new man, like a young married footballer returning from his first World Cup.

In *The Iliad*, marriage is all about honour and wives are the spoils of war. Achilles and Agamemnon are given beautiful trophies like Chryseis and Briseis. When Agamemnon decides he wants Chryseis, he starts bargaining with her father to give her up. Famously, things didn't end so well for Agamemnon, although you could argue that being killed by his thoroughly cheesed-off wife added to his fame.

Of course, it's hard for us to empathise with these patriarchal ciphers, but King Priam of Troy is a legend in the modern sense of the word. First, he had to deal with loads and loads of kids as a result of his wife, Hecuba, being one of those super-fertile types who just loves popping them out. Fifty of them in her case. A man with so many offspring can at least hope to be taken care of in his dotage, but one of his sons, Paris, instead of pursuing a sensible career, became a total player and started the Trojan War. Priam had had an inkling (a prophecy – the ancient equivalent of a funny feeling) that he would do something like that and had tried to do away with him at birth, but couldn't go through with it because Paris was such a sweet baby. Later on, with the war in full swing, his beloved son Hector is killed and Priam makes himself a hero to emotionally open men everywhere when he goes crying into the Greek camp to beg Achilles to return his son's body to him.

Old Priam prostrates himself before Achilles and delivers a speech of tremendous emotional power – 'I bring my mouth to the hand of the man who killed my son' – invoking Achilles's love for his own father. Both men weep. Achilles takes the old man's hand and agrees a truce of eleven days so that Hector can be given a proper funeral. Achilles says:

'How did you find the courage to come here all alone and meet the eyes of me that have killed your sons? Your heart is truly made of iron! Come here, sit on the throne and despite our pain, let our suffering lie quiet in our hearts. For no profit comes with lament.'*

So the Greeks invented bromance too.

Does Paris's early life remind you of anyone? The royal parents fearing that their boy will grow up to do something terrible so they abandon him on a hillside, only for a good-hearted type to rescue him and raise him as a normal bloke? Who may or may not go on to kill his dad and have sex with his mum? Yes, it's Oedipus. The unluckiest husband in history. The man in whom destiny, free will, sexual desire, power and self-awareness got so jumbled up that it took Freud to start unpacking his baggage, and every man after him to wonder what to do with all the stuff that the father of psychoanalysis had unpacked and left lying around where anyone might trip over it.

My personal journey around the Oedipus story began when I watched Pasolini's *Edipo Re* as a student and immediately recast every character from ancient myth as a sexy Italian with oily hair and heavy eyeliner. Now, years later, after having a son and learning about psychoanalysis, I know that the love between mother and boy is a chthonic fire-bolt that cannot be contained and will surely send hot ripples of trouble down through the generations as each baby boy becomes a man and tries

---

* http://www.grethexis.com/achilles-stunning-encounter-priam-king-troy/

loving women other than his mother. And then, if he's lucky, becomes a father who loses his wife to the love of another baby boy. Drama.

But how did modern marriage as we know it really begin? If all we had to go on were paintings like Chagall's *Russian Wedding* or *The Village Wedding* by Samuel Fildes, we would think matrimony in the past was a cheery and natural coming together of two rosy-cheeked youngsters in love. A blushing bride and her handsome groom, carrying her parasol for her – the first in a life-time of helpful, supportive acts – skip along a country lane flanked by their proud parents and a retinue of merry country folk bearing baskets of delicious food and flowers. Off the newlyweds go to their fecund new life together, with not a care in the world.

Of course, the reality for most men and women was more like one of the late works of Goya or a particularly toe-curling Paula Rego. Until shockingly recently (the divorce act of 1856 was when things slowly began to improve), most marriages were arranged, mercenary and physically dangerous.

The patriarchy was awful for both sexes, and daily life for men before the Industrial Revolution was hideous unless they were in the top 1 per cent, which even then didn't protect them from frequent illness and bereave-ment. The pernicious effects of religion, feudalism, illit-eracy, militarism and poor public health left ordinary men fighting a losing battle for their lives and freedoms, and we know they often took it out on their wives and children, just as they had seen their fathers and their fathers' fathers do. What an epic, viral tragedy it was for most boys to grow up without the safety of a kind, healthy home and a mother who would live to see him grow up. To see his mother beaten, ruined by childbirth and running scared; to have a father with no outlet for his sadness but alcohol and spousal abuse. The legacy of violence and repression is a ruinous, inherited disease. And let's not forget, most marriages were between children or teenagers, which is a recipe for disaster even now.

Here's what marriage looked like before the late twentieth century:

Whether rich or poor, a family with daughters needed to marry them off as soon as possible, to leverage social power and get shot of an expensive drain on their finances. So children were betrothed to one another even before they could understand what matrimony might involve. Which is probably just as well, given that it meant, for the girl, enforced sex and dangerous pregnancies and the theft of any property she might have, along with the right to keep her own children should the marriage fall apart. For the husband, the situation, while less horrific, was cold. Marriage held no promise of love, friendship, good sex and affection, and the frustration many young husbands felt when this reality dawned on them was plain to see in the emotional and physical punishment they meted out upon their dependants. A groom was just a pawn in the transaction between the two sets of parents.

None the less, there is such a thing as true love. And kindness. And devotion and sweetness and cheeky giggles and small kisses and funny secret faces and the knowledge that you would lay down your life for the person you adore, and that, when they are gone, you would burn down the world to see them one more time. The great love stories of art and literature have endured through all the miseries that our attempts at civilisation have wreaked upon us. And all the best romances (Romeo and Juliet, Anna Karenina, Antony and Cleopatra) depend upon mean, venal or jealous others as the obstacles that show the strength of true love. In reality, for every dramatic, fictional archetype there were many happy marriages: loving partnerships full of affection where no one jumped in front of a train.

History has left us powerful love letters between truly happy couples – from Mary Wollstonecraft and William Godwin to Ronald and Nancy Reagan – which glory in the strength and delight of two human hearts brought together in marriage. Even volatile loons like Frieda Kahlo and Johnny Cash give us pure, noble devotion in words like these, to Diego Rivera and June Carter respectively:

'You deserve a lover who listens when you sing, who supports you when you feel shame . . .

You deserve a lover who takes away the lies and brings you hope, coffee, and poetry.'

'We read each others [sic] minds. We know what the other wants without asking . . .

You still fascinate and inspire me. You influence me for the better. You're the object of my desire, the #1 Earthly reason for my existence.'

That said, histories of marriage in England are the saddest books you will ever read. Women surrendered their freedom to a stranger with no legal recourse to help if anything went wrong. The slightest misstep, like spending time alone with another man, or showing too much independence from her husband, could – and often did – end in imprisonment or committal to an asylum and never seeing your children again. Ironically, this reign of terror against the mothers of England didn't even result in their menfolk being happy, because the grooms themselves would have been the product of similarly dysfunctional families, and were probably accustomed to seeing their mothers (if they saw them at all) punished. The trauma for these boys must have been very great too. Towards the nineteenth century, as marriage and divorce law became separated from the church and more records of marital dilemmas were kept, we read accounts of many men succumbing to severe mental illness by the pressures of an unhappy home and society's pressure to conform. Losing so many children to infantile disease must have been the last straw for these troubled homes.

Surprisingly, it could be even worse for the rich than for the poor, because there was more money and social shame at stake if the 'love' match misfired. Working-class couples could drift apart, quietly commit bigamy or just disappear from each other's lives if things went wrong. The extended families weren't risking being brought down by their scandalous offspring.

Generally the privileged lived, as they do now, in a bubble, where extramarital flings and private lives were cushioned somewhat by having numerous rooms in various grand houses to repair to (although shame and sexual humiliation did of course still lead to a good deal of nastiness). There was a time, in the 1930s, when London high society was full of openly adulterous marriages. Divorce was still expensive, so spouses turned a blind eye to affairs. When Edward VIII and Wallis Simpson began their entanglement, she was very much still married to her second husband. He not only tolerated the expensive diamond jewels Edward gave his wife, complaining only about the cost of insuring them, but let their besotted royal visitor make himself at home, pouring drinks for guests and acting like the man of the house.

But for the middlingly well off (a tribe whose numbers grew stratospherically in the nineteenth and early twentieth century with the Industrial Revolution), making a good marriage was the single most important aim for any young person.

How many innocent young men recoiled in anxiety, on their wedding night, as Ruskin was said to have done? The famous pre-Raphaelite bro let his marriage go unconsummated for years and, according to his wife Effie, it was all because 'he had imagined women were quite different to what he saw I was ... he was disgusted with my person'. When their marriage was finally annulled, Ruskin admitted to the court that 'it may be thought strange that I could abstain from a woman who to most people was so attractive. But though her face was beautiful, her person was not formed to excite passion. On the contrary, there were certain circumstances in her person which completely checked it.'

History does not record what exactly it was about Effie Gray's naked body that repulsed him so much, but whatever it was, the blame can be laid squarely at the door of a thousand years of paintings in which women's genitals are either obscured by tendrils of climbing plants and wisps of muslin, or, if exposed, look like those of freshly scrubbed babies. And goodness knows what the virgin bride thought about her husband's 'person' . . .

The nineteenth century was a prime time for sexual alarm. In 1880, forty-year-old John Cross had been married to George Eliot (the cleverest and richest woman in Britain at the time) for only a few days when he leapt out of the window into Venice's Grand Canal. Why he did it has been the subject of much speculation, ranging from horror at having to sleep with his ugly wife, inability to cope with her wedding night demands, to heatstroke or just plain mental strife. The 'ugly and horny' line of argument tallies with the obsession with Marian's (let's not call her George) looks and was perpetuated by Henry James, who damned with faint praise when he wrote that her charm and intelligence made her face seem less wretched to the point that he found himself 'literally in love with this great horse-faced bluestocking'. Evidence of Marian's romantic fervour is found in her numerous unrequited passions and her strident writing about relationships and not wanting 'light and easily broken ties' but rather the kind of hot, risky love affair that means she won't necessarily be 'invited to dinner' by polite society but will be sharing her best life with the man of her choice. So it's typically bonkers and upfront of her to marry a much younger man she had only known for a short while after having lost her long-term life partner, George Henry Lewes.

Perhaps the reason for Cross's leap was the desire to do something – anything – to make him look as superhuman and crazy in love as the heroic Lewes, an example of top Victorian totty who proves that nineteenth-century husbands weren't all stiff collars and butterfly collections. Few men have devoted themselves so selflessly to their famous wife's fulfilment of her vocation. Denis Thatcher? Prince Philip? Pah! Lewes was a total catch and even now, despite the wispy chinstrap beard and comb-over that makes every nineteenth-century man look like an Amish swinger, is pretty gorgeous. He was a polymath: an actor who starred in Charles Dickens's am-drams; a decent writer on art, philosophy, politics and science; a charismatic South London Bohemian who was fine with his wife having a couple of kids with his best friend, staying married to her but moving out of their (presumably book-lined and charming) West London pile. He supported, edited and loved Marian, and when London society wouldn't accept them, took her off to Weimar to hang out with cool Europeans who were chill with their set-up. What a fine man this iconoclastic wit, critic, amateur scientist (hurrah for amateur scientists – where are they now?), biographer of Goethe, poet and playwright was. A jewel among Victorian husbands, whose typical responses to 'masculinity in crisis' were all sorts of weird behaviours not including being nice to women.

A hard act to follow. What could Marian's second husband do but autodefenestrate to prove his worth?

In the twentieth century, divorce laws, sex education and a burgeoning awareness of psychology were able to help heterosexual couples deal practically with the vicissitudes of married life. A good deal of shame around sex and money still kept many troubles unspoken (as they do now), but we start to see a proliferation of guidebooks and magazine articles aimed at helping young couples navigate the mysteries of each other's minds and bodies. Dr George Napheys's popular *The Physical Life of Woman*,* published in the 1870s in America, dropped the bombshell that there was no physical way a young groom could prove whether a bride was a virgin on her wedding night. A big stride forward in gender relations, only somewhat undermined by his going on to say that

---

* https://archive.org/stream/thephysicallifeo24001gut/24001.txt

the only real way to tell whether she has been interfered with already is to gauge the purity and innocence of her demeanour.

Napheys, a well-travelled and highly qualified and experienced medical doctor, doesn't limit his advice to physical matters, but weighs in on the emotional too:

'Love is one thing to a woman, another to a man. To him . . . it is an episode; to her, it is the whole history of life. A thousand distractions divert man. Fame, riches, power, pleasure, all struggle in his bosom to displace the sentiment of love . . . But a woman knows no such distractions.'*

Well, by 1919 she certainly did. Advances in education, voting rights and medicine ushered in a new age of equality that took men by surprise and gave women a taste of the power they had waited so long for. Something had changed for men, too, as we see from a new emotional honesty in their letters home from the battlefields of the First World War. In the face of terror at the front, outpourings of love and affection for their sweethearts and children came thick and fast, in terms that a generation before might have considered the stuff of silly romance novels. Suddenly, men were talking about what kind of husband they wanted to be: how they yearned to love and support their wives, and, crucially, to have fun and make a happy home with them.

* Ibid.

Letters home from the trenches are surprisingly honest about the trauma of war, and some historians now believe that men's identities as husbands, sons and fathers, bolstered by the ability to write and receive personal letters from home, enabled them to cope with the psychological hell of trench warfare.

In a series of emotionally candid letters and diaries collected by his grandson, the journalist Toby Helm, Cyril Helm, an army doctor with the Yorkshire Light Infantry speaks of the 'unimaginable' feelings he had as he sat 'listening to shells and wondering how long there is before one comes and finds your hiding place'. After watching his 'friends picked off one after the other' he confesses that: 'At times, when I realised all those, my pals, had gone, I nearly went off my head.'[*] Some twentieth-century writers on shell shock and trauma in the First World War have even likened the experience of being stuck in a trench as the closest men ever got to the constrained domestic lives of Victorian women, their imprisonment resulting in a kind of 'male hysteria'.[†]

In their less hysterical moments, we find ordinary men acknowledging with great insight the way grief might affect their wives and also how marriage has helped forge their own identity. These moments make for some of the most moving letters home from the front. Private

[*] https://www.theguardian.com/world/2013/nov/03/ww1-memories-imperial-war-museum-share
[†] https://encyclopedia.1914-1918-online.net/article/subjectivity_and_emotions_great_britain_and_ireland

Albert Ford wrote to his wife Edith just before going over the top in October 1917: 'Know that my last thoughts were of you in the dugout or on the fire step my thoughts went out to you, the only one I ever loved, the one that made a man of me . . . Do think of me in the future when your grief has worn a bit, and the older children, I know won't forget me, and speak sometimes of me to the younger ones.'*

It's not surprising that the outbreak of war brought with it a spike in hastily arranged marriages as a vain defence against the disposability and meaninglessness of life in the age of mechanised mass warfare. When the survivors finally made it home, records show a huge increase in divorce. This was partly because, in the men's long absence, women began to seek comfort elsewhere, and also because the trauma of war was more than innocent young marriages could support. The same phenomenon can be observed after the Second World War; although most of these post-war divorce petitions were instigated by the husbands, who perhaps found their wives had strayed in their absence, returning married soldiers were often riddled with venereal disease after using prostitutes while abroad, so were the wounded party in more than two senses.

By the late 1940s, divorce proceedings were quicker and more straightforward than ever, with special

* https://news.sky.com/story/dear-heart-love-letters-from-the-trenches-released-10767255

dispensation for a speedy passage through the courts for returning soldiers. Finally the world was waking up to the fact that it is unfair to trap young people in unhappy marriages when they might live happier, more useful lives as divorcés. And women, who had proved their independence, skills and financial worth, were no longer as dependent on their husbands for money. As one woman from that era put it, in Julie Summers's excellent history of returning soldiers, *Stranger in the House*, 'The boys who came back were not the boys who went away. They were men. Different men with different ideas; and they found us different, too. The shy young girls they left behind had become women – strong, useful women with harder hearts and harder hands, capable of doing jobs that men never dreamed women could do.'

So in those bleak post-war years, marriage was in crisis again. Add to the pain and shame of divorce, the emotional and physical effects of war on people's homes and bodies, and we remember how awful civilian life could be. Violence, alcoholism, family courts that didn't put the child's true wellbeing and wishes first, and financial hardship all contributed to a pretty bleak domestic scene that made alcoholism and suicide among men and women common.

However, from these mean ashes, a new era of the husband emerged. The modern married man as we know him today was born. In the 1960s, the academics John and Elizabeth Newson published their seminal works of family sociology in which they interviewed hundreds of working- and middle-class British families about what life looked like at home.

Men were showing (and admitting to) a commitment to parenting that would have been unthinkable in previous eras. One farmer's wife, Mrs Ross, said of her husband:

'Oh, he'll do anything for either of them – he always has – bath, change, feed, wash for them. They're all their daddy. There's a scream when he goes and a howl when he comes back in case he's going again.'*

While the legendary Mr Ross was something of an extreme case, we start to see men pitching in with childcare as never before. The remit of the married man was changing and, while there was still a gender divide and some anxiety about what was proper and improper for a man to do (a father taking his son fishing: fine; a father soaping up his toddler daughter in the bath: nope), many husbands were showing a real interest and emotional investment in home life. Cooking, taking the baby out in the pram, looking after all the children for a day while mother goes out to work or socialise, doing the supermarket shopping, helping children with their education ... and, crucially, valuing themselves for it. Or at least not hiding it from the world: dads pushing prams became a fairly normal sight by the 1970s.

From 1977, when I was born, until now, there has

---

* John and Elizabeth Newson, *Patterns of Infant Care in an Urban Community* (London: Pelican, 1965), 138.

been a steady upward trend of men doing more domesti-cally. Sure, the steepness of their learning curve was mocked in classic 1980s film and TV comedies like *Three Men and a Baby* and *My Two Dads*, but in reality, family life was more egalitarian than ever (which is to say, not very – women were still assumed to be the chief bum-wiper and skivvy – but attitudes were improving).

In 2003, paid paternity leave was introduced in Britain, and that long-overdue legislation reflected a few decades of men realising that looking after children is actually a really nice thing to do. Maybe even nicer, say, than sitting in a smoky pub watching darts on telly and feeling cut off from your wife and child's affectionate, playful, adventurous life at home. Men were reflecting on the emotional distance and helplessness around the home of their fathers and grandfathers and they wanted to change. Because how can you feel good about your-self if you can't cook dinner or soothe the child you would lay down your life for? The internet made work-ing more flexible, and also opened our minds to differ-ent views and ways of life around the world, and by the turn of the century it was quite unremarkable to see a man working on his laptop in a café with a child in a pushchair by his side.

Actually wearing the baby on your body in a sling has proved the last frontier of new fatherhood, however. When Piers Morgan said it was emasculating for a man to wear a papoose, I was surprised to hear several educated male friends admitting that they too felt a bit silly and 'off' doing it. Still, the patriarchy has been chipped away at with great enthusiasm when it comes to the modern man about the house.

However, in some homes even now, as we approach the second decade of the twenty-first century, gender roles are firmly lodged in the Edwardian age. In one house in my street, the sixty-year-old retired husband goes for lunch at his club every day when his wife is not home to cook for him, rather than having to make something for himself. Our houses are one hundred and twenty years old, and I can't help musing what their original inhabitants would think of us modern married residents. I don't suppose a retired gent in 1910 would have had to go out for his lunch, because there would always be a servant to cook for him. There were so many people to look after a middle-class, middle-aged married man when our lumpy, redbrick semis were snazzy new-builds. Now the servants' quarters have been repurposed to become home offices for part-time PR consultants and separate bedrooms for each tiny child; and the husband of the house is expected to pick objects up off the floor as well as cook his own lunch and earn lots of lovely money. I don't know how he does it!

Husbands and Their Mothers

'She's the greatest woman I've ever known. Nobody else,
except my mother, comes close.'

Johnny Cash

Wasn't it Freud who said:

> 'Your mama is so big and fat that she can get busy
> With twenty-two burritos, but times are rough.
> I seen her in the back of Taco Bell with handcuffs'?

And did he not go on to say that he also saw her

> 'On a cliff butt naked, tootin' on a flute
> Ridin' on a horse drinkin' whisky out a boot.
> She's got the teeth and the wings of an African bat,
> Her middle name is Mudbone and on top of all that
> Your mama got a glass eye with the fish in it'?

Possibly that was the awesome nineties hip-hop group
The Pharcyde, but the deep meaning behind these words

is straight out of 1930s Vienna: the mother figure as the repository and focus of all the shame and power a man can know. The Pharcyde go on to imagine your mama's 'glass titty/Filled up with Kool-Aid just for the kiddies' – an image that strikes at the heart of what's problematic about boys and their mummies: those lovely boobies suddenly turn embarrassing, and the desire for them something to be laughed at and feared.

It's no surprise that all great art from Sophocles to The Smiths is teeming with problematic mothers. Every marriage is as well. Not long ago I was at a wedding where, just as the vows were being exchanged, the mother of the groom leaned over and whispered something to her son. I spent the rest of the day desperate to know whether it was: 'You don't have to do this, baby' or, 'There's spinach in your teeth'. And at another marriage I attended, a country wedding with the church doors wide open on to the meadows beyond, one dear-departed mother's absence was felt keenly by all present. When a pretty butterfly flitted in and flew in circles around the bride and groom just as their marriage was being blessed, one of the more suggestible gentlewomen of the parish cried, 'That's her!' Of course she did. Because mothers are everywhere. In our imaginations, our dreams and our selves.

My son is still little, but I do sometimes fantasise about his wedding day. While statistics suggest that he will marry a woman, in my dreams he has forsaken me not for a version of myself with brighter eyes and shinier hair, but a gorgeous young man who also adores his mother and will remind him to love, honour, obey and live very near me for ever as long as we both shall live. And at that ceremony someone will read, in a booming voice, from Luke 11.27: 'Blessed be the womb that bore thee and the paps that thou hath sucked'! And my son and I will have the first dance together.

And that is how messed up and extra a mother's love for her son is. So it's no wonder that once a man grows up and finds a partner, whether male or female, the infamous figure of the mother-in-law looms large.

Take Winston Churchill. How would his young bride, Clementine, have felt had she known that, before their marriage, Winston asked his mother for some wedding-night sex tips? And then reported back not only to his mummy, the prolifically romantic Lady Randolph, that thanks to her wise words they had 'loved and loitered' to great effect, but also wrote to Clementine's mother too, about what a 'delightful occupation' sex with her daughter was. Cringe! Doubtless this has much to do with posh boys being complete strangers to their parents in the good old days: the intimacy of a modern mother–son relationship would make such an interaction horribly transgressive.

I know one mother of a teenage boy who felt it incumbent upon her to explain the difference between porn sex and real sex, to try to save him and his future partners from the time-honoured tradition of rookie lovers poking things in and out of their lasses and then feeling confused at the lack of transcendent joy on the feminine face. I don't know exactly how that chat went, but he didn't immediately leave home or chop his ears off. Maybe he has become a supreme lover, wise beyond his years? Maybe he thinks of his mum every time he's in bed with a girl? Who knows! The point is, a mother will happily leap over any social boundary there is to help her boy succeed.

Having a mother-in-law may be a well-worn comedic trope, but as with threesomes and eating sandwiches on the beach, the clichés are all true and most people try it only once or twice. The smothering love of a husband's mother can be majorly problematic in a modern marriage, especially when a man's wife and his mother are very different sorts of lady, or think they are.

'My wife would cut my bollocks off if I ever compared anything about my mother to her,' chirped my friend Ali, merrily, when I asked him about mum-on-missus relations. 'Both are super-strong women and are slightly wary of each other. It's always a strained relationship, I think.' He fears that his wife could be resentful if his parents 'have a difficult old age and become dependent on us . . . the old people's home will beckon before that happens. A John Betjeman poem springs to mind.'

One of the problems for a grown man trying to manage the relationship between his mother and his wife is accepting that his mother is also a wife herself. In fact, a woman in her own right. Viewing your mum as an adult, independent lady can be complicated because it means seeing her not only as that awesome being who can park a minivan and arrange an overdraft, but as a person who wants to have orgasms and is scared of dying, and other dangerous and yucky things.

'In other words,' explains my Freudian friend Joseph, 'to see her as a separate person engaged in relationships that do not centre around her son. This goes to the very core of the classic male narcissistic defence (against the loss arising from separation from the mother) of regressing to an Eden-like state, where you are together and alone with a mother figure, bound in perfect fusion, as if she is really a part of you (i.e. your rib).'

More, please. Because this is my favourite kind of talk:

'Well, falling in love can present a man with the fantasy that he has discovered a way back into this conjured-up, primal place of perfect union and bliss. But with marriage, under the spell of the serpent (that tempts him into sexual exploration of his partner) and with every bite of the apple of wisdom (as he acquires forbidden knowledge of his wife's secrets), he is drawn to the inevitable confrontation with the God-like internal father figure, that angrily shatters the illusion of flawless fusion and expels him once more into a world filled with hard work, pain (children and taxes) and death. Which leaves him in a state of shame and the need to defend himself. The shed becomes his palace. The car becomes his power. The garden becomes his kingdom. The challenge of marriage is to wean oneself once more from the ever-caring maternal figure and to learn to love and value your partner as a separate individual.'

My mate Tim can relate. He married young and has just celebrated twenty-five years of wedded bliss (two cats, many lovely holidays and no children by choice). He happens to have a very successful mother, to whom he – and the rest of the world – looks up. 'I was always aware of my mother having a life outside of the family and being known by a lot of other people because of her job, so I've been able to hold both concepts of her – mother and individual – in my head without thinking about it.'

I run the Churchill sex-tips story past him and he looks horrified. 'I'm hugely uncomfortable discussing sex and it's been referred to obliquely only a couple of times in forty years. I never spoke to my parents about that sort of thing and only properly introduced my wife-to-be when we got engaged.'

So what do you talk to your mum about?

'Botany.'

Is that all?

'No, of course not.'

What else?

'Ornithology.'

Perhaps because there are no children and perhaps in spite of it, or quite possibly because they've never traded sex tips, Tim's family are one of the closest I've come across. Not a weekend goes by without an expedition mounted to some place where husband, wife and mum-in-law can indulge their common interests, and as the Ps get more aged, Tim and Mrs Tim are a constant, helpful presence in their lives. Mother and son are certainly very pleased with each other, and in the adjoining villages in which they live, are following a well-trodden path of conveniently oppressed, happy familial love.

Interestingly, both Ali and Tim were taught from an early age to be independent of female domestic care, and were washing, ironing and tidying up after themselves by the time they left home. 'I recall asking to be taught how to sew when I was about eight and since then I've done a lot of my own repairs and still do,' Tim tells me. And hurrah for that mother, because we all know what happens when a mummy loves too, too much – she raises a spoilt, helpless man who can't even boil an egg. Traditionally, fathers might teach their sons the important 'life skills' of bonfire-making, fish-catching and pint-downing, but how many men are cast out into adulthood with no idea about the really useful everyday stuff like making jam and removing bloodstains? These sort of skills are super-attractive to prospective partners, after all, so unless mothers want their sons to be alone for ever, they should really consider teaching them.

The Husband in Waiting

'The longest sentence you can form with two words is: I do.'

H. L. Mencken

Once upon a time, a man's life didn't really begin until marriage. Bachelorhood was generally a sexless (or pox- and guilt-ridden) state, and a chap was still under the thumb of his parents until he set up home with his bride. Unlike the modern male's long spate of post-adolescent, premarital independence and fun, women were a mystery to our unmarried forefather, as he had no female friends and his sisters bathed in nighties. Marriage was expected, desired and encoded by state and church as the only proper way to live, so for the young swain still living at home and being told that interfering with himself would make him go blind, getting hitched must have seemed like a one-way ticket to a warm bed and ordering whatever you fancied for dinner each night.

Still, those of an enquiring nature did wonder about the possible downsides, as a young Charles Darwin demonstrated in his list of the pros and cons of wedlock. He wrote in his dairy:

Marry:
Children ... Constant companion, (& friend in old age) who will feel interested in one, —object to be beloved and played with.—better than a dog anyhow.—Home, & someone to take care of house—Charms of music & female chit-chat
Not Marry:
Freedom to go where one liked—choice of Society & *little of it.*—Conversation of clever men at clubs— Not forced to visit relatives ... fatness & idleness— Anxiety & responsibility—less money for books[*]

In the end he did choose to chance cohabitation over getting fat and hanging out with a dog, and the love between him and his cousin Emma Wedgwood evolved into a long and happy union.

Whether Darwin's proposal to Emma took place in a flourish of roses and bended knees or was more of the 'Cuz, bring it in' variety, history does not relate. But we know that for many young suitors, the proposal itself is as big a challenge as the prospect of signing away one's freedom.

As Bertie Wooster, that serial altar-dodger, observes in *Right Ho, Jeeves* when his newt-fancying pal Gussie

---

[*] https://www.darwinproject.ac.uk/tags/about-darwin/family-life/darwin-marriage

Fink-Nottle doesn't have the guts to propose to Madeline Bassett, 'Reflect what proposing means. It means that a decent, self-respecting chap has got to listen to himself saying things which, if spoken on the silver screen, would cause him to dash to the box-office and demand his money back.'

Yet feverish romance of a cinematic nature is exactly what many future wives expect from a proposal, even now when most couples have reached the openly farting and no blow-jobs stage of cohabitation by the time they agree that getting married would probably make sense tax-wise. I know one down-to-earth thirty-something couple who both, but especially the husband, are as cynical and gruff as any self-respecting modern pair. One day as the wife and I were hanging out, getting to know each other in the normal way (swapping drug and birth stories) I asked her how her husband popped the question. Well. She began to describe an epic saga – misty-eyed on her part, wide-eyed on mine – on a par with most arcane medieval chivalric romance: mysterious twists and turns, a woman alone in the forest, horses, and a series of trials. First, she was presented with a white pony and brought side saddle to a bucolic, grassy sward. A trail of rose petals had to be followed into a wood, where a series of clues were laid out for her to solve. Each correct answer won her a piece of a jigsaw puzzle and finally led her (and I think there was a maze involved at this point?) to a prettily laid table with champagne and all that but also a jigsaw puzzle, with the couple's faces printed on I should think, but I can't remember the details because by that stage I was questioning reality itself. With the deft application of the missing puzzle pieces, milady spelled out the fateful words 'Will You Marry Me?' And husband-in-waiting popped up out of the bushes to hear the answer.

Unbelievably, that's not even the most extreme proposal I know of. A friend of a friend was whisked off by private jet for what appeared to be merely an exciting day out, only to land on a tropical island and find an entire surprise goddam wedding laid out for her. Dress, mother, cake, friends . . . how could she say no? I must have been sweating visibly as she told me this shocking tale because she was quick to assure me it was 'like a dream' (in a good way) and 'a real fairy tale' (not one featuring Bluebeard, I presume). I suppose what first attracted her to the billionaire who laid on this instant wedding must have been his impulsive, *carpe diem* approach to life, so it was all in keeping.

Even chaps without private aircraft tend to feel they must do more than bang a ring down on the breakfast table before leaving for work. They must 'set the scene' using items generally unfamiliar to them, like pretty cushions, fluffy blankets or a non-pork-and-ale-based picnic for a proposal designed actually to please the one being petitioned. One chap I know dug a fire pit in the garden and invited his almost-fiancée to sit by it and roast stuff. Another wanted to do it on a beach at sunrise, so had to keep his girl up all night and not let her go home to bed.

Like a bold, solitary questor, the would-be fiancé plans his campaign alone. He won't brainstorm it for months with his friends; he hasn't spent weeks furiously watching rom-coms for tips; he isn't texting his bestie all day saying, 'Ooh, I'm really going to do it! So excited!' because the serious business of proposing is the act of a lone wolf. Most don't even ask the father's permission these days for fear of offending.

Most husbands report the ring burning a hole in his pocket (after having done its job of burning a hole in his bank balance) while waiting for the right moment. And he could be waiting some time. 'She was in a stinking mood the weekend I was planning to propose,' confided one friend. 'I had to wait for her to stop scowling and chill out, so we'd have happy memories of it.'

For men in the public eye, a proposal at home, away from prying eyes, is obviously preferable. Prince Harry reported that he took Meghan by surprise by whipping it out in the middle of a chicken-roasting session at home, and she barely let him get all the words out, let alone the ring, before giving numerous hearty Yeses. George Clooney says he set up a complicated 'ring reveal' involving a matchbox and an unlit candle, but when he sent Amal to go and get a light she seemed bemused by finding a lump of metal in there: 'She pulls it out and she looks at it and she's like, "It's a ring" – as if somebody had left it there some other time.'

I once arrived at a country-house hotel for the weekend and noticed a young couple bearing all the classic marks of two about-to-be-engaged humans. He scurried around looking flushed, distracted and cheeky and kept tapping his pocket, which on its own might just suggest he'd trousered a few hot sausages from the breakfast buffet, but combined with his girlfriend's gleaming manicure, numerous photo-ready outfits and dreamy look, told everyone that troth-plighting was on the cards. That evening they had arranged to have a special dinner served in a private nook away from the main dining room, and the waitresses were all skittishly toing and froing with flutes of champagne and knowing winks. The young lovers were surrounded with red roses, enclosed in their own world, their hopeful faces bathed in flickering candlelight, when the lusty swain got down on one knee and opened the little velvet box. It was a beautiful moment. I know this because it was exactly then that I had to chase in after my youngest child who had taken a wrong turn on the way to the bathroom and was crouching under their table yelling, 'Big big poo, Mummy!' Like the feckless owner of a nasty dog, I suppose I smiled indulgently as I carried my stinking offspring away, knowing that what all the roses and champagne are leading to is, after all, just the hope that one day you will be blessed with the chance to repeatedly wipe muck off a miniature version of your lover's bottom.

But why does a marriage proposal require such fanfare after all? And why does the modern chap go along with it? It's the first and last bit of over-the-top romance a man is really allowed to go in for, and it's possible that he rather enjoys this patriarchy-sanctioned excuse for pretty event-planning. It can't be gay to get deep into selecting the perfect hue of rose petals for the table if it's all in pursuit of a bird, right? And even if he does think it's a bit daft, there's a grave reason for it, after all – it's the final hurdle in the heroic battle to winning life's ultimate prize. Misjudge the proposal and you could end up broken-hearted, a genetic dead-end or, worse, a sad internet meme.

Also, men love a good set of instructions, and there's a fairly well-trodden series of boxes to tick for a classic proposal, starting with the location. This should ideally be somewhere cute, photogenic and a bit out of the ordinary. One friend of mine was whisked off to an adorable medieval country cottage where her boyfriend cooked her a delicious meal and cracked open a fine bottle of wine. Sitting beneath the beams and old plaster walls, he appeared distracted during dinner. She began to wonder if something romantic was afoot. He was definitely on edge: couldn't meet her eye, pushed his food around his plate. Finally he came out with it: 'Sweetheart, there's something I want to say to you but I'm not sure how. And I just don't know if you want me to. OK, here goes. Look, there's a massive spider on the wall just above your head.'

And then there are those chaps who never get round to asking at all, because marriage just seems like a 'piece of paper'. One's inclined to think that these guys are actually massive commitment-phobes or have a secret family in Grantham or hate their girlfriend's mum too much to go there. So I was pleased to meet one very thoughtful fellow (cohabiting and co-parenting happily with his partner) who told me why he's the non-marrying kind:

'Marriage has been used as a subtle but powerful mechanism to bind a couple in the eyes of others, law and even God. Each of these "witnesses", I feel, is meant to wake a different type of fear in us to keep the knot tight once the "magic" is gone (fear of social rejection, of legal difficulties, of financial struggle, and in the last instance, fear of disappointing God and falling from his grace). I personally don't think love or commitment should require any witnesses other than those who love each other and share that commitment. I don't believe signing a paper, making a vow or throwing a party makes two people more engaged, more in love, or more connected. I believe that that intimate bond is precisely the most private and voluntary event and that there is really no point in making others part of it.'

Which is actually quite romantic.

Husbands up the Aisle

'The love of a husband and wife is the force that welds society together.'

St John Chrysostom

'I took one look at her and said, "This is it. I'll be back for you. Stick with me, kid, and you'll be farting through silk".'

Robert Mitchum on his wife, Dorothy

Marriage is the last remaining patriarchal structure from the good old days of women being owned by men. So it's a happy twist of fate that, today, so many men get totally owned by their weddings. It's no sexist cliché to say that even the simplest register-office-then-lunch affair is likely to have a man wondering if his wife-to-be actually hates him and his entire family. Because, like it or not, a wedding represents all the hopes, dreams and idiotic fantasies of our status-hungry lizard brain. Whatever a woman's biggest fear is (Poverty? Pretension? Extravagance?), there's an expression of it in the weave of the burlap cloth surrounding each mini flowerpot on the top table.

Where does this leave the husbands? It's testament to the emotional import of wedding planning that when I asked around, no man would admit that the wedding his spouse planned was a hideous ordeal and he hated every second of it. Most confess to turning around a few years later – once the real marriage is under way and turns out to have nothing to do with mini shortbread hearts and tables named after Winnie the Pooh characters – and wondering why on earth they thought spending twenty thousand pounds on a party was a good idea (although let's remember the deep philosophical truth in Jerry Seinfeld's take on going out to buy a hyped-up, over-advertised, fancy new car: 'I know it's a lie. But on my way to getting the thing, it's not a lie yet. I'm excited and I'm happy.'[*])

Yet for most men, capturing their quarry – I mean joining together in holy matrimony – feels like a remarkable achievement. Possibly the only real achievement of their lives. From Winston Churchill to Justin Timberlake, husbands seem to view themselves as foul beasts who somehow managed to fool a princess into loving them. 'My most brilliant achievement was my ability to persuade my love to marry me,' said Winston. Then, a century later, Justin catches 'a glimpse of her when she

---

[*] *Comedians in Cars Getting Coffee*, created by and starring Jerry Seinfeld, Season 10, episode 1, Netflix 2018.

doesn't see me looking and I have this moment where I'm like – "if you never make a good decision . . . if you only make bad decisions for the rest of your life, you made one really good decision",' which is just a modern, slightly less patriarchal, spin on the 'I'm a loser, she's an angel' trope. Which, as we all know from rom-coms, is as politically fraught as it is disingenuous.

I love asking men about their wedding day because some very funny looks come across their faces. For women, on the whole, wedding recollections revolve around how the florist nearly screwed up, and she fell out with her mother over the seating plan, and she couldn't breathe in her dress. Grooms, by contrast, recall a day of genuine emotional intensity interspersed with occasional shocks. But more than with any other subject in this book, most of the husbands I asked about their nuptials clammed right up, muttering platitudes like, 'It was a lovely day' or, 'My wife looked beautiful. I think everyone enjoyed the wine!' and looking around for the exit. Even when pressed, specific details were rarely forthcoming. Had they forgotten it all, as trauma some- times wipes the hard-drive? Did they love every detail so much, from the corsages to the mini, heart-shaped coffee spoons, that they daren't sully it with the retelling? Or are they perhaps aware that the whole affair was so laden with significance for their other half that they're not quite permitted their own version of the day?

What if his favourite memory was not all the expen- sive frippery but the funny moment when the food ran out, or someone making up a silly song? Some husbands would balk at admitting this but one man I know, Harry, will happily reveal all with the voluble enthusiasm of an eight-year-old recounting his first trip to Legoland. His infectious love for the day (and his wife) is a pure joy:

'Our wedding day was amazing! We planned it together in three weeks, which sounds stressful but in fact it was pretty easy. We didn't have time to get stressed or be indecisive and lucky for me we were and are so in love and my wife is so unsuperficial that we both knew it would be a special day. We didn't have much money so we knew it would be modest. We settled for a room above a pub. We ended up running out of food so my dad came to the rescue by going to Sainsbury's for bread and cheese. We had friends to do the flowers; my friend drove us in his parents' bling car; my band played and we got friends to make party playlists on iPods. My dad had written a song about us for everyone to sing along to. Our friends and family also helped clean and decorate the room the night before. They also did a whip-round and chipped in so we had our wedding night in a London hotel. It was a great day . . .'

Of all the crazy destination weddings and three-day island extravaganzas it was this wedding that kick-started the happiest marriage I know. These two are so in love it radiates from their grins and giggles even now, many years and children later.

Even a man who had a relatively modest but more traditional wedding (eighty people in a country church followed by a marquee in the garden – it was nice; I was there) says that if he could do it all again he'd just do a small ceremony and lunch in a favourite restaurant, because 'it all seems such a waste of money and fuss. But I didn't know what being married really meant then, aside from putting on a big event.'

So what does a wedding actually mean to a man?

'I think the public avowal of commitment bound up in a legal/religious contract is an important demonstration of mutual faith. But of course, avoiding inheritance tax for your partner is very important as well,' James, a sensible chap, told me at his thirtieth wedding anniversary party recently. My mate Harry had a bit more to say on the subject:

'Being married compared to just being together does feel different. I am proud to say my partner is my wife (not in terms of ownership!). There is a certainty with it that I find comforting and there is a kind of clarity to it. It is a statement – this is my partner for ever. It is an immediate "we" not a "me and". There is a lot of stigma when it comes to marriage these days in that people think it is this ancient ridiculous institution that is in some way now obsolete, especially considering how many end in divorce. I get that, but I think in an equally positive and negative way it makes people more likely to work at it. This can obviously be seen as marriage being a kind of trap but I also think it equally helps people to not make such rash decisions in ending relationships when that's not necessarily the right thing. I think for some people like me that marriage is important and has intrinsic value. It is similar to the point of a wedding really: there is something very human about publicly declaring to everyone that you have a lifelong partnership.'

It takes more than two to make a marriage, according to a wise uncle of mine: 'I think marriage is important for the commitment one makes in front of witnesses whose job – at least in my view – is to help the couple uphold those commitments.' Which reminds me of the speech the wife made at the thirtieth anniversary party mentioned above. She, glowing with love still like a young bride, although with several children, houses and dogs under her belt now, stated plainly that either she and or her husband would die first, and it was a great source of comfort to know that we, their assembled friends, would be there for the one that remains alone. Cue much eye-dabbing from the ladies and some nervous, jokey heckles from the gentlemen. As you would expect when someone tells the truth about love.

Husbands in the Nursery

'Sherman made the terrible discovery that men make about their fathers sooner or later ... that the man before him was not an aging father but a boy, a boy much like himself, a boy who grew up and had a child of his own, and as best he could ... adopted a role called Being a Father so that his child would have something mythical and infinitely important: a protector, who would keep a lid on all the chaotic and catastrophic possibilities of life.'

Tom Wolfe, *Bonfire of the Vanities*

When it comes to babies and children, the modern husband is expected to be all that a woman is and more: always loving, selfless, eager to change nappies and happy to forget about a social life. Even Prince William does his royal duties, bleary-eyed from self-confessed sleep-deprivation, and David Beckham says he feels physically ill when he has to leave his kids. The modern father really is bucking the trend of millennia of patriarchal rule by giving up all those fun freedoms, isn't he?

And he's loving every minute of his new milky, snotty existence. Although in fact, as we know, he isn't really loving it that much. And neither are mothers. Everyone would prefer to be out having a drink with their best friend than staying home wiping liquid poo off an angry baby's back. Of course they would. But luckily, something happens to the modern parent's mind when a child is born: a madness that is one part self-sacrifice, one part exploring your limits as an animal that can function on no sleep (or sex or clean sheets) and many parts wondering about subscribing to *Which?* magazine.

I know very well how parenthood feels for women. My friends have talked of little else for the past ten years, and when we're not physically talking, even the most chat-room-phobic of us will stay up late at night scrolling the Mumsnet message boards until we've reached the critical number (34) of descriptions of the exact weird problem our child is having. Our husbands talk about the details of baby-wrangling much less. But is that because they're busy doing and talking about other stuff? Or are they less interested?

What do husbands really feel when they are up at two in the morning and again at four and six with a crying baby and a cross, ill, hysterical or depressed wife? Are they closing their eyes and imagining the little rounded form of their newborn is in fact their childhood teddy? Or a fierce wild boar cub that they've just taken down with their bare hands? Are they fantasising that their partner, hunched over under the duvet pretending to be asleep, is really the hot Italian mum from *Call Me By Your Name* and she's about to spring up and make him an apricot tart for breakfast?

Joseph, a psychoanalyst friend of mine, says that when his wife had babies he began to envision himself as a sort of container, holding the chaos and madness of his new family in a sturdy embrace. This was one of my favourite conversations ever, because his emotional, artful chat is like slow poetry and he did this lovely womb-y, bowl-ish gesture with his hands to show me what he meant. It was, he said, in his lovely gentle therapist's voice, a distinctly motherly feeling of being a still, round, empty thing that will support new life, in contrast to the traditional penetrating dynamism of masculinity. I love conversations like this. It's so interesting to talk about yourself as a bowl.

Back down on earth, I notice on my travels around North London and occasionally beyond that, increasingly, you see men with babies everywhere. A generation ago you might have found dads swarming the playground on a Sunday morning while Mum got the lunch started, but nowadays a husband on his day with the kids is likely to be found lunching in a grown-up restaurant, going for a run with his off-road pram, or checking out an exhibition or movie with the baby strapped to his chest. He has found that living your normal life doesn't have to stop when you're carrying a bag of nappies. In fact, many women consider their husbands to be much better at this than they are, and envy the gung-ho way a father will take the kids off to the zoo at four p.m. with no supplies other than a Twix and a credit card. Because even if they come back starving and covered in wee, they will all have had the most amazing time.

You also find the modern husband propping up the bar at the local pub, as per his forefathers, but now with a kid or two in tow. Extended licensing hours, the food revolution, the smoking ban and pubs becoming generally less disgusting have been a lifeline for dads, as Neil, a writer with a baby boy, told me:

'One difference parenthood has made to me is that I never drink a beer stronger than 5 per cent on my daily afternoon visit to the pub. But I like to get out of the house . . . maybe chat to the barman. The baby likes it too.'

I've yet to see a big clan of young husbands all having coffee or going for a walk with their kids, but that says more about the way men do friendship than fatherhood (meet up with six other guys at ten a.m. for a milky drink? Just to talk? Errr . . .)

However, proliferation of child-friendly cafés, and the rebirth of urban coffee culture, means that a man can work in a hearty breakfast or nice lunch amid his child-care duties. There are places springing up all over Europe which combine a children's playroom in the back with a hip coffee place in the front. And as it's only really men – those great collectors, cataloguers and perfectionists – who are mad about sourcing the 'ultimate' coffee, it's safe to assume that it's dads who are driving the market for cold-brew, single-estate arabica served by chaps with special beards and raw linen pinnies. And if their children can go off and tinker with some wholesome wooden toys, all the better to avoid the stigma of giving their kid a phone to play with while they drink it. Everyone's a winner. In fact, in my neighbourhood, a hugely successful iteration of this concept was set up a few years ago by a local dad, who used to run a mums-and-babies music group in the church hall, but saw a gap in the market for something less noisy and more welcoming to men. His trendy, industrial-style café has become the focal point for weekend dads, full-time fathers and pre-work parents for miles around.

Leaving the café and moving on to the park, we find that while dads still congregate in the playground, they do it in a different way to mothers. It's not, for them, an excuse to get stuck into a major gossip session with their windswept fellow parents. Instead, they get actively involved in the character- and muscle-building activities of their little darlings, suggesting new routes up the climbing frame and encouraging them not to be scared while hanging from the monkey bars by a single tiny, slippery hand. They're here to put that kid through her paces, or it's a waste of everyone's time. In the event that their offspring don't need them, or the husband is just having a bad day, they might simply stare mournfully into space like Superdry-clad menhirs (not looking at their phones of course, because that would show they hate their child and hope it spends its life in prison). *Fathers in the*

Playground: A Study in Ennui is the imaginary artwork I have often composed while staring at these men as my own children fall off the monkey bars. It's a sort of L. S. Lowry/Otto Dix mash-up. Most affecting.

The only place I never saw a sullen or overly pushy dad was in the playgrounds of Oslo, where I spent a few months when the children were small. The men in that famously family-friendly city seemed totally at ease with themselves: gossiping a bit, playing a bit, eating, chilling out on benches being hot and liberal, clearly just the right temperature in their Didriksons parkas. In fact, I thought Norwegian husbands were the happy princes of modern manhood, until I read Karl Ove Knausgård's *My Struggle*.

Knausgård, the Viking rock god of European letters, writes about marriage and fatherhood with disarming candour. His prose studies of hellish children's parties and awkward toddler music groups are classics that will have anyone who has ever held a nappy bag nodding in bitter recognition. But in the final instalment of his six-volume, gazillion-word, novelised autobiography, he reveals all the not-so-cool things he does when alone with his children. He is often so distracted by thinking about his writing, that he will suddenly freeze in horror while dawdling in the newsagent's or strolling along a canal having a fag and think, 'The children! Where are they?'

He describes collecting the kids from nursery when his wife is away, and the two youngest falling asleep as soon as they get home. Like every parent of toddlers, he wrestles with the maddening dilemma of whether to sacrifice the peace to be gained now by letting them slumber on to escape the carnage they will wreak later when they're still not ready for bed at eleven p.m. He's chill. He's desperate. He's a modern father. So he just lets them sleep. And miraculously, unbelievably, they sleep through the whole evening and night! He simply transfers them into their beds, not waking them to feed them supper or change their clothes. Half the parents reading this will be punching the air and calling him a legend, marvelling at this never-before-seen twist of glorious fate. The other half will be clutching their pearls at the thought of such a ballsy rejection of routine.

Karl Ove admits to shouting at them, taking out his frustrations on them, and often just finding them really annoying. He smokes, he sticks them in front of the telly when he needs to work. He wishes they'd shut up. Most parents would feel or do the same sometimes, but few dare to admit it, let alone commit it to print. It takes a man very much in touch with his notions of self-doubt to say these things. And Knausgård is openly ashamed of himself almost all the time, as he repeatedly writes and says in interviews. It's his thing. But having been an adoring, committed, thoughtful, self-aware father for many years, his children know how fiercely he loves them.

One can't help wondering how the modern husband's exposure to the vicissitudes of parenting affects marital relations. We are all familiar with the hilarious advice columns of the 1950s where women were told to shield their men from the blood, sweat and tears (and mashed banana and depression) of raising children. One matron I know, now in her nineties, is horrified that young women don't always wear makeup for their husbands. Do men mind the warts-and-all approach to co-parenting? Is the chummy 'realness' to be gained from checking each other's stretch marks a fair swap for the dream of coming home to freshly washed children and a perfectly primped wife who just can't wait to serve up a dinner and watch while you read the paper? Aside from the actual miraculous horror of watching his lover give birth, the daily pressures that having a baby puts on a marriage is quite startling to many young husbands. As one dad told me, a few years after the birth of his last child:

'You see each other differently as partners as you see each other being parents, and you don't have nearly as much time for each other as partners. Having less or no sex for a while is a part of this, but the biggest struggle is remaining affectionate and supportive with each other whilst trying to always do the right thing with the kids. I admit on some level I got – and still get – jealous of the kids and the connection they have with their mum. I think you constantly have to check yourself when you are feeling like you need attention.'

Once the baby stage is over, and you're both occasionally washing your hair again, a new menace looms for the unsuspecting husband: the average toddler's passion for imaginary games. The playroom is a torture zone for many men because of the pressure to perform. Of course, plenty of women hate it too, but mothers who spend more time at home won't feel as guilty as a husband for loathing make-believery because they know they're pulling a twelve-hour solo shift every day, so avoiding pretending to be a rabbit for half an hour doesn't seem like such a crime. I know this feeling very well because although I do like imaginative play, put a board game in front of me, especially a long one like Monopoly or the mind-numbingly pointless Sorry! and my entire consciousness shrinks to one point: a single, obsessive, animal desire to flee. My famous ability to sit in a room doing nothing for hours on end thanks to my peppy internal life vanishes. I hate my family. I hate myself. I get narcoleptic yawning fits, a cognitive fug and am quick to explode in rage. I never, ever feel like this in any other situation. And this is how husbands who hate being rabbits feel. Candid Harry admits as much:

'Childcare can be boring. I don't enjoy playing very much, which my wife seems to do with such ease. I find it hard to be on their level and pretend to be a zombie/monster/pirate with enthusiasm. My wife spends more time with them too so she has more practice and she knows their triggers better than me. I have many male friends who have the same problem with play. My mind wanders sometimes which makes me feel bad when I realise they are trying to get my attention. I spend less time with them which undoubtedly means I know them less so I am not in tune with their needs in the same way she is. This is particularly frustrating when I am playing with them and can't work out exactly what they're after – then she comes along and sorts it out straight away which can be very annoying!'

Harry is so open about this and everything that I thought I'd ask him about the last taboo of contemporary fatherhood: discipline. Most men hate talking to me about this. All my girlfriends get straight on the phone in tears when they have spanked their five year old or told a tweenage daughter that she will never have any friends if she continues to act like such a bitch. It's what we do with shame: we reveal it, hoping for a conspiratorial, if lower-case, 'me too'. But the legacy of generations of birch-wielding gents dies hard and most husbands are scared to analyse their anger. Nonetheless, I knew if anyone would speak the truth about how it feels for a big man to scream at a little toddler, it was Harry:

'As far as discipline is concerned I do find it hard. I am a softie and I don't like telling them off, because it gives rise to a part of myself which sadistically enjoys it. This is hard to explain without sounding like an abuser but I think it makes you aware of the power you have and must control. It also makes you aware of how careful you have to be, and gives you an idea of why some people are abusive. It doesn't justify it at all but you realise we all have it within us – some more than others,

I guess. The point is, kids are extremely testing and getting the balance right when it comes to being loving and supportive whilst being able to discipline is no easy feat. The worst is if my son has been naughty during the day and I have to come home from work and reinforce the fact that he is in trouble and might go to bed without a story. And I love story time!'

Listening to him talk like this reluctantly called to my mind some of the times my husband and I have told our children off. I tend to hiss long, unkind, solipsistic sentences beginning with 'Well I never imagined, when I had children . . .' It's a bit nasty. But my husband has a different tack: he never overdramatises, never threatens; just tells them what they've done wrong and which of our useless punishments they can expect to receive ('No, Daddy! Don't take away my sustainable oil-based agave-sweetened chocolate spread!' This sounds like weak right-wing satire, I know: they won't eat Nutella since being poisoned against it by their right-on mates.) But the thing is, due to their manly, caveman voiceboxes full of gravel and old fish bones, when a man is upbraiding a child he makes a sound that is LOUD AND BAD. Men can so easily sound powerful and scary even when they don't really mean to (just listen to them shouting at the telly when the cricket's on), and I think all fathers know this and it makes them feel horrible.

One man who knows this better than anyone is the brilliant novelist Edward St Aubyn. I recall an interview with him in which he spoke about disciplining his children.* In case you haven't had the rare pleasure of reading him, his autobiographical novels manage to describe child abuse and drug addiction with such intellectual charisma and dark humour that you want him never to stop, which is quite weird and amazing. Years of trauma followed as an adult but, now he's a sober and loving dad, how does he cope with having to give his kids what-for if they do something really awful? Well, he relies on a great deal of rational talking, explaining and negotiating until finally, possibly, if he really has to, he tells them off. What a silk purse of a dad his beastly experience has made him.

That interview was given when his children were small, but goodness knows what mean things they say to him now they're teenagers. Because when the little darlings get tall and hairy, the hapless husband must face a whole new set of internal threats: now his kids will openly tease and denigrate him, sometimes in a vernacular he barely understands, and they'll either find his anguish and confusion jolly funny or just another example of why they think he's an idiot.

* https://www.newyorker.com/magazine/2014/06/02/inheritance

Husbands in the Dressing Room

'Without black velvet britches, what is a man?'
James Branstom, *The Man of Taste*, 1733

You have only to glance at the advice column in *Country Life* to know that questions like when it's OK to wear a tweed tie, and whether a tailcoat should always have Petersham silk lapels, are keeping the modern gent up at night as frequently as ever. These are not issues a wife can give advice on. He's on his own here. Now you might think, looking at more mainstream new sources, that today's man has other worries. You might also assume that once married, such concerns are forgotten, because there's nobody his wardrobe must perform for. But my research reveals that married men – especially those of a certain age – are very much preoccupied with correct standards of dress.

From the husband whose wife (me) once tried to buy him a shirt with a pocket, to the dandy who regularly put the bins out in a scarlet, sequinned morning suit but patiently explained to someone suggesting a pair of shades (also me) that he would never wear sunglasses because 'they're so over the top, don't you think?', men are frequently amazed at the silly items their womenfolk expect them to put on. These sartorial 'lines in the sand' define a vital part of every man's identity, and it's not something he's willing to give up upon marriage. The rules of the wardrobe are so subtle as to be invisible to most women. To us, the uniform of a husband at ease resembles that of an eight-year-old boy off school with mumps. So it's comforting to look a little deeper and learn that those threadbare trackie-b's have been carefully chosen for the particular way in which they fall over the top of a greying tube sock.

More mature husbands – those who have never worn elasticated-waist jersey exercise slacks – might have a quite different view of what sportswear is, as evidenced by a conversation I recently had with a 92-year-old lady I know. She was merrily reminiscing about her late husband, a stylish chap born in the 1920s, and the various codes of dress he and his fellows adhered to. These were only the ones she knew about, of course: there were surely many more whose secrets remained in the dressing room.

'Shoes. They must be black. Brown are only for sport.'
Sport? What, to be worn with shorts and a T-shirt?
'*No!* With tweed of course.'
Ah, that kind of sport.
'And a Viyella shirt with the Harris tweed jacket, of course, with twill or cord trousers for casual wear. And

you know, he would polish his shoes every single evening. He never asked anyone else to do it. He took great pride in it. It never came up that I should do it. It was his thing. Ties: a sporty one (tweed) might be worn on the weekend, or even on a very relaxed day, a knitted one. But there was never a day when a tie wouldn't be worn. Unless you were playing tennis.'

If this sounds like a bit of a bind, remember that this lady's mother-in-law (class of 1900) put on a hat after breakfast and didn't take it off again until she went upstairs after tea to dress for dinner.

In those days, you couldn't possibly pretend not to care about such things. Now there's a whole generation of men who happily proclaim a hatred of fashion and clothes shopping, and wish they could leave it to their wives (but don't quite dare – see the breast-pocket outrage). It's a generation of chaps between approximately 10 and 100, including a friend of mine in his early forties who informs me 'I gave up on "fashion" a long time ago as all men should by their late twenties at the oldest.'

Husbands may not trust their wives to buy their clothes, but they certainly hope to get their approval. 'I'd like it if my wife expressed more of a view about what she does like me to wear, actually,' said my clothes-mad friend Andre, who has the money to attire himself very grandly, and does, plus has the honed physique to carry off the most fitted of Italian suits. 'I am confident in all clothes and think I can "do" quite a lot of looks successfully, which I find fun. Dressing well is important!' I ask him what he thinks when he clocks another dandified chap cruising down the street in a carefully put-together get-up. 'I think well done – provided I like his particular aesthetic. I might be pejorative if I think the bloke looks like a tool, but not for having made the effort to look like a tool.'

Got it.

Another husband I know – a well-turned-out sort who goes to the gym every day and never lets his hair accidentally grow cowlicks or rats'-tails, laments that his wife doesn't always credit him for his efforts: 'I wouldn't mind if a lady told me I looked nice. It's nice to know you've still got it now and then. Even if I am getting on a bit, I try and look after myself and stay clean and groomed, but I feel like it's not appreciated sometimes . . .'

Most married men seem to aim to look neutral and unremarkable, and become so lazy with their wardrobe that they fall into the sad old cargo shorts and khaki T-shirt look, so as not to look too – you know – feminine and vain, shall we say. But of course they're only human and they want to be loved, just like everybody else does, and that means being admired. How many have sat watching the magnificent bird of paradise on television, strutting its gorgeous plumage in front of that bored, dowdy female, and felt a secret admiration for his bravery in getting out there with his best clothes on and doing a little dance for his lady in that specially prepared forest clearing? It's just not how most men were brought up, though, is it? Because ever since Englishmen stopped wearing big curly wigs, silk stockings and makeup, the patriarchy has saddled them with a huge anxiety about the decorative and pretty side of life. We humans are the only animals on earth where the female gets more dressed up than the man to go out to dinner.

The way men get around this societal pressure to look boring is either to ink their skin with swirling baroque pictures of angels, animals and stars or, if they're not the tattooing sort, jazz up their wardrobes with a floral blouse. I've long been mystified by the vogue for grown men wearing flowery shirts. Who could have foreseen a thriving market (some thirty years old, according to the chap I asked in the basement at Liberty) in shirts made of that pretty Tana lawn stuff your granny used to make up into summer skirts with a bit left over for a baby's smock? How did this happen? Is it some kind of complex double helix of style, referencing both the decorative sensitivity of the Arts and Crafts movement and the bold athleisure of 1950s surf culture? Was it that their wives had bagged (begging + nagging: such a fun skill) them to wear something nicer than a football shirt so they rose up in rebellion and sartorially said, 'Try walking down the street with this on your arm then, darling'?

I asked a leading fashion journalist for her opinion on this phenomenon.

'It is essentially a way for men, generally middle-aged extroverts who think they are hilarious, but spurn high fashion, to feel festive and express their "fun" and "rock and roll" side in a safe and unthreatening way,' she says. 'They might be worn by a man who says things like, "Why do women get to dress up and not men?" Until recently, men's fashion was quite plain, compared to say the 1970s when everyone wore floral shirts, but now there are currently a lot of high-fashion print shirts from Prada and Gucci, which are flamboyant and cool, but they take some daring and styling expertise. The Liberty style shirt has evolved as a very specific style signifier which is generally not considered cool. It's Jonathan Ross and James May territory. It's dad fashion par excellence: dads in floral shirts, or DIFS if you will, the male equivalent of mums in leather trousers.'

They look worrying, to me, those big men covered in rosebuds, because it's such a conservative, uptight way of looking pretty, compared to the full-on fairy-tale dressing of 1970s rock gods, 1980s clubbers or glorious trad-trannies. Like pure, tailored angst.

Then I remembered that I actually know someone who wears these pretty blouses. A beefy, alpha male prone to fits of putting his point across quite enthusiastically. So I asked him why he favoured florals. Horrified at the mention of his past misdemeanours, he assured me that he hasn't worn them for years ... it was just a moment of crazy, youthful experimentation, like shearling jackets or neon socks. On marrying, his wife had quickly put a stop to it and now he realises that they are a sinister cover for aggressive men who want to hide behind something inoffensive-looking while acting like beasts. Which makes perfect sense, actually. So much so that I'm even a bit scared of grannies in flowery skirts now. Not to mention babies.

Shoes can't scare me, though, and I've heard a lot of women say that they notice a man's shoes before anything else, so husbands-in-waiting take note. Yes, lads, when a lady's gaze drops down below your belt on meeting you, it's just to check for black Reeboks.

A married relative of mine is an extremely careful and subtly creative dresser (think silk socks with vintage desert boots maintained weekly with a special set of brushes) and he shuddered when he recalled the day his wife suggested he might 'wear trainers' for his hour-long walk to work 'for comfort reasons'. 'I have to draw the line somewhere,' he says in genuine horror at the thought. He is a man who enjoys maintaining his clothes and accessories with archaic tools like thread and boot polish, and subscribes to the make-do-and-mend mentality that was rife when his gorgeous 1930s style gear was first in fashion. He does however admit that his wife – a rosy-cheeked country girl who mostly stays out of town while he sashays around WC1 not in trainers – has 'shaped how I dress to a degree, through approval and input'. As he has grown up, he has fixed on a striking personal style that really suits him and is half Renaissance prince and half accessible, non-threatening office-mate. 'I joke that I dress for my public. There's an element of vanity, for sure. I do notice others dressing well. It's more than putting on a suit: there's a schtick that goes with it. I also notice dressing badly. A bit of me dies when I see someone outside their home wearing tracksuit trousers.' (I bet if he saw gorgeous Tan France from Queer Eye walking by in his jodhpur-style apricot sweats he'd come back to life, though.)

Lewis, a business owner with a super-cool wife who always looks as if she buys her clothes from a secret shop in Goa that I will never find, agrees that a wife's opinion is not to be sniffed at. 'I quite like it when she appreciates how I am dressed. I value her opinion on that far higher than anyone else's.' Does he think dressing well is important?

'Increasingly yes – in a kind of dress-for-the-role-type way. It is a means to an end.' Until his business took off I'd never seen him in a suit, only the hoody and flip-flops uniform of the overgrown teenager. But the day I encountered him fresh from some industry event, his form poured into a great suit, I had to do a double take. He says he's developed an eye for 'clean, smart, well-shaped tailoring. When it feels sharp, generally so do I.'

Suits are interesting, aren't they, because they're so boring. Even a pink velvet one is an ironic reference to the inherent, essential boringness of its nature. But is this boringness a cover? Grayson Perry writes in his unmatched meditation on masculinity, *The Descent of Man*:

'Men who really want to camouflage themselves when getting up to nefarious activities wear a grey business suit. I think a primary function of their sober attire is not just to look smart, but to be invisible in the same way that burglars often wear hi-vis jackets to pass as unremarkable "workmen". The business suit is the uniform of those who do the looking, the appraising. It rebuffs comment by its sheer ubiquity.'[*]

As everyone knows, there's only so much a suit can do for a man if something frightening is growing on his face. And beards are something on which wives tend to have extremely strong opinions that only the boldest husband dares to flout.

One southern Mediterranean gent of my acquaintance revealed to me that in the barber shops back home, men get the edges of their beards threaded for precision. (NB: threading is an extremely painful and gorgeously precise method of hair removal favoured by Ottoman ladies with big, amazing, swoopy eyebrows. But I'd never heard of men doing it.) Right up to their eyes, he says, in some particularly hirsute cases. Now this particular fellow could grow an absolutely stonking beard and yet he forgoes it for the sake of a happy marriage. Blissfully wed for many years to a woman who knows what she likes, he understands that facial topiary is an easy way to please his beloved and possibly the key to their longevity as a couple:

'The main thing I do when I want to impress my wife is shave. She does not like me with stubble.'

[*] Grayson Perry, *The Descent of Man* (London: Allen Lane, 2017), 50.

There's a fine line (particularly when threaded) between beard, not-beard and stubble anyway. It's an ontological minefield. A friend of mine thought her husband – one of those big, blond types who looks like he's just turned on to Kentish Town Road from an ice floe in twelfth-century Svalbard – was just a stubbly, chilled-out bloke who didn't shave much. Until she realised that he wouldn't be shaving for their wedding day, and therefore actually self-identified as a man with a beard.

Historically, it was women who were the drivers of men taking up the fragrant self-care we now associate with male grooming: aftershave and deodorant were pushed in the early twentieth century by wives who wanted their husbands to be a bit less rough and ready, not by men out to snare a lady. And initially, husbands resisted it, saying it was unmanly. Thankfully those clever people in marketing have been able to reassure men that spraying on a bit of Lynx is an act of hyper-masculinity on a par with having sex and fighting a lion at the same time.

The last word on the subject of husbands and their looks goes to a friend of mine, Ali. He looks like the ultimate country gent, is always clean-shaven and instinctively knows when not to wear a tie. He gives me to it straight when I ask him for the secrets of his dressing room:

'Do you dress to please your wife?'
'No.'

'What kind of clothes make you feel confident?'

'A nice whistle.'

'What do you think when you see a man who has obviously put a lot of care and attention into his outfit?'

'Twat.'

Choreplay

'I got the blues thinking of the future, so I left off and made some marmalade. It's amazing how it cheers one up to shred oranges and scrub the floor.'

D. H. Lawrence

'There was no need to do any housework at all. After the first four years the dirt doesn't get any worse.'

Quentin Crisp, *The Naked Civil Servant*

I never feel more alarmed over the state of gender relations than when women are scoffing at their husbands' attempts to do housework. It's easy to understand why the issue is so acrimonious and politicised but it's still shocking to witness a generally loving, well-balanced lady go purple in the face and hiss 'Just fucking leave it – I'll do it' when her husband starts to clean up in the kitchen. The husband, an otherwise confident, grown-up fellow – a lawyer perhaps, or a prime minister – will mewl, 'OK, sorry, thank you, if you're sure', before backing out of the room. And then, I assume, heading out to kill a prostitute.

Every household will have a different version of this involving more or less hissing, but I don't know a family where this has never happened and the underlying principle is always the same: some damn fool of a man has had the brass neck to suggest he might be able to clean something properly! So the husband thinks he must be no good at it. So next time, he doesn't offer. And the lady gets cross about it. And they *never have sex again.*

It's a pretty bad scene. It's also an intriguing manifestation of the afterlife of millennia of female domestic enslavement: women using their shackles to bash their gaolers' heads in. And, in a way, bashing her own head in too, because no wife really wants to be a housework expert, let alone one so good at it that she gets promoted to the lonely role of arbiter of other people's cleaning skills. However, something strange happens to a couple, in between the blushing engagement photo and the row in the kitchen ten years down the line. Strange and bad for husband and wife alike. That something is modern patriarchy and it's no good at all for husbands (unless they are into being adult babies). Speaking of adult babies, I've always wondered: do the fetish 'mummies' diverge as much in their childcare routines as real mothers? Do some leave their hulking tots to cry? Feed on demand or timed feeds? Do the babies themselves have a preference, seeking sub-sects of their kink where they will only be fed every three hours then left to self-settle?

Back to housework. There's no doubt that who does more chores is a major source of 'grrr' for many couples. And it's obviously something we are, as a culture, keen to understand, because there's a constant stream of data coming from media-friendly sociology departments trying to calculate the precise damage to a marriage for every hour a dirty pan is left in the sink.

I recently wrote an article about this for a feminist website, based on a new bit of research claiming that couples who share housework are happier. I no longer had the original report to hand, so went online to try to track it down. What were the first three results for my search of 'housework and marriage statistics'? 'Couples Who Share the Housework Are More Likely to Divorce' (the *Telegraph*); 'Domestic Equality Makes Couples Happier' (also the *Telegraph*) and 'Marriage Is Better If You Outsource Housework' (*UK Business Insider*). Diverse conclusions like these say a lot about the relatively new science of quantifying happiness and wellbeing, and also make me think that when it comes to marriage and family life, people lie a lot. We all do: we make things seem worse than they are to get sympathy and laughs, or sometimes put a rosy blush on a stinking situation in the hope of shrugging off the shame that goes along with disappointment.

Husbands are often accused of proudly advertising every bit of domestic work they do, and indeed over-estimating the amount of it. Wives meanwhile probably underplay the jobs they do at home because so much of the minutiae of drudge-work is done thoughtlessly, in a couple of seconds, while holding a baby in the other hand and talking on speakerphone to the office. Call that 'multitasking' if you want to put a professional-sounding spin on it, but for many women – whether housewives or salaried workers who do most of the childcare and cleaning after coming home from their paid jobs – this is known as the 'mental load'.

The mental load is a cruel invention of the modern woman's brain that looks like an endless shopping list or receipt of all the many little tasks, reminders and jobs that need to be done on rotation for ever until everyone leaves home or dies. Sometimes it's not just a list of jobs but a complex matrix of conditions and potential outcomes and sounds a bit like this: 'If the baby sleeps until three I'll chop the onions for the bolognese before she wakes up then it'll be quicker to cook later when the others are hungry, but if it's raining and we can't go to the park after the school run then we might go out for tea instead so they won't be hungry so soon, so instead of doing the onions now I could wash my hair but then again the noise of that might wake the baby but if I don't I'll feel gross so . . .' And that's what's spinning around in a woman's head when her baby is asleep. I have found no man whose head sounds like this, and if it did he'd probably go straight to the doctor for a mental-health assessment.

If a husband is looking after the baby on his own and the baby is asleep, he will rest if he's tired, or do some work or get stuck into a book or some telly. If he's holding the baby upright for five minutes after its feed it's unlikely he will have a J-cloth in the other hand and get ahead with the chores by wiping down the worktops. And I don't think he'll bend down to pick up socks and Lego from the floor either, in that moment. Because he's busy.

I say all this not because I'm a horrible sexist but because every single married man and woman I have ever asked says it's true.

I did eventually find the study I was looking for, in which sex and washing-up boffins revealed that couples who share the housework report more intimacy, more often. Which sounded like old news to me. This was the thinking behind the 'porn for women' gift book that did the rounds a few years ago, showing handsome hunks doing the vacuuming, polishing silver and giving hot quotes like 'as long as I have two legs, you will never take the bins out'. It suggested that husbands must perform certain challenges – a sort of domestic *Krypton Factor* layered on top of an ancient chivalric code – in order to be admitted into the bedroom by the gatekeeper of conjugal activity, their wives. But the authors of that paper, 'Declines in Sexual Frequency among American Adults, 1989–2014' found that the real reason is that couples who share chores are better at communicating and sharing

– two rather important factors in maintaining a peppy love life.*

My own research supports the importance of 'choreplay' too. My most romantically active friend has a totally egalitarian breakdown of domestic tasks in his happily married home, and enjoys a free and fair dialogue with his missus about what route their adventures should take next, in and out of the bedroom.

But the majority of husbands I spoke to about housework painted a rather terrifying picture of the role of domestic work in their lives.

One of my grandest friends, Alastair, is a classically handsome fellow in his thirties with a pack of posh dogs and a huge and beautiful house. The type of chap who is usually busy playing the violin beautifully or dashing off a thank-you letter to a head of state when you go round to see him. His career is sickeningly successful; he's the life and soul of the party, has thick floppy hair, and is universally adored by children and ladies alike. But get him talking about folding towels and you see a shadow fall across his rugged face:

'They just don't look like towels when I fold them,' he laments. His wife, he admits, finds housework 'a constant job'. Alastair, however, tends to wait until the proverbial and actual laundry bag is full.

---

* J. M. Twenge, R. A. Sherman and B. E. Wells, 'Declines in Sexual Frequency among American Adults 1989–2014', *Archives of Sexual Behaviour* (2017), 46: 2389–2401. https://www.ncbi.nlm.nih.gov/pubmed/28265779

'For my wife, it's constant. I do have a list at the back of my mind of things that need to be done, but it's more about finances and schools and things. I don't have a constant need to do all the tidying. I resent that women want us to be maids of all work, which we are not and cannot be. Ironing – what's the point? It doesn't look good when I do it. If I look at a room and worry about what needs to be done, I can't work. And I need to work.'

Did I mention he's an artist?

Another mop-dodging husband of my acquaintance, Neil, learned early on in his marriage that any attempt by him to tidy and clean would only enrage his neat-freak bride, because he wouldn't do it to her standards. He told me he wishes he could help her out but knows better than to try. With young children and two busy jobs to wrangle, this couple are frequently frazzled, yet tidying is actually therapeutic for his wife, to the extent that she will come home from a hard day at work and spend an hour doing it to wind down. How do you feel about that? I ask Neil. 'It pisses me off.'

Occasionally, however, the elasticated hygienic shoe-cover is on the other foot. Enter the super-charged husband for whom housework is just another thing to excel at and do full-throttle. Ted is one such guy, who already, with his twinkly good looks, honed gym bod and open-hearted, hippie-meets-serious-philosophy-type dude mentality, is most women's ideal man. But he also loves tidying. Loves it! And food shopping, which he doesn't wait until the cupboard is bare to do, and doesn't consist of him buying only mustard and chocolate (actually I don't know that for sure, because I've never been to his house, but he looks like he eats vegetables). Plus he's not averse to wiping up spills, ironing and organising the ephemera of family life. He doesn't see it as a woman's job, so when he's not busy raising daughters or reading about women's emancipation, he's probably giving his skirting boards a right seeing-to with a Dettol wipe. Incidentally, Ted is a majorly macho man. Too macho even to like football, which he considers a babyish diversion that turns men into toddlers. ('Waving their arms in the air, shouting, taking their tops off . . . ugh. Little boys.') He's into extreme sports that can kill you. He drinks, smokes and shags. He's so good at his job that he's in possession of the kind of fortune that means he never has to get busy with a Dettol wipe again. Yet for him, housework is man's work.

Then there are the husbands who will do one job – only one – and make it a badge of honour to do it better than anyone else. Ironing and washing-up seem to fall into these categories. Once upon a time, a bloke in love with a crisply pressed trouser seam used to be a military man or a tailor, but these days is as likely to be a musician, like my friend Sally's husband, or my cousin Octavio. These two set aside a weekend afternoon every week to get to the bottom of their ironing pile, and not because their wives have told them to. 'It's meditative,' says one; 'It's satisfying,' says another. 'You're so shit at it,' my own husband would probably say, grabbing the iron from me and taking over.

One gent of a certain age I spoke to, who looks as if he should have a butler, adheres to his favourite household task – washing-up – like a spiritual practice. After dinner, everyone in his family knows to leave him alone. 'It's my time,' he says. 'The radio goes on, the kitchen is peaceful, and I love the feeling of the warm water and suds on my hands.' Almost like a stressed-out mummy sinking into a hot bath at the end of a trying day. Has anyone ever tried combining the two, you might wonder? Yes they have, but it's a story from my university days so disgusting that I'm not yet ready to tell it.

So let's end this glimpse into the laundry basket of married love with an altogether more wholesome tale. Two of my dearest friends, Mr and Mrs Piper, have been married for twenty happy years, but I had not thought, until recently, to question who wields the hoover in their home. When I finally asked Mr P about it, our conversation about domestic life had me on the edge of my seat. Maybe I'm naïve but I did not expect a liberal, creative fifty-year-old to drop a bombshell like the fact he had never, ever baked a cake until a week ago. I thought everybody with a kitchen and a mouth and a child had baked a cake, but how wrong I was (and I've since learned that another fifty-something husband of my acquaintance is similarly inexperienced; when I asked him how, why and wtf he said, 'Err . . . I don't like cake').

Here's the deal: throughout their marriage, the lady of the house has been in charge of catering and cleaning. Both partners have busy jobs, but for reasons ancient and modern, it was the woman who took responsibility for keeping everyone fed and scrubbed. Mr P, a highly educated feminist who is soppy about babies i.e. A Good Man, didn't feel he was much good at all that stuff, and was a bit fearful that he would do it all wrong. So life went by, with Mrs P cooking ever more exciting recipes, redecorating the house, and hiring and firing all the cleaners, gardeners and cat-sitters that a long marriage works its way through. Then suddenly, in middle age, things in Mr P's brain began to change. He realised he didn't feel comfortable in his own kitchen, with its mysterious cupboards and drawers, and wondered at the pleasure his wife got from being there. He, traditionally, had found meaning in interests outside the house: work, exercise, politics and philosophy. But it wasn't making him happy, so he got mindful. Got meditative. He began to expand his inner horizons to encompass the weighing scales on the kitchen counter. Could cooking food actually be fulfilling? Could he too rejoice at the way it feels under your hand when you add egg to creamed butter and sugar and the wooden spoon starts dancing on marshmallow rather than grinding through grit? The week before my chat with him, he had made his first cake. It was pretty good. He needed to ask his wife for a few tips, and these she gladly gave, and he received, with no teasing, shame or resentment. And that is what grown-up husbanding (and human-ing, and loving) looks like.

Husbands in the Kitchen

'The life of the cook was a life of adventure, looting, pillaging and rock-and-rolling through life with a care-free disregard for all conventional morality.'

Anthony Bourdain, *Kitchen Confidential:*
Adventures in the Culinary Underbelly

Ever since women were liberated from the kitchen and permitted to suffer outside the home as well as in it, men have expressed themselves at the stove in all sorts of unusual ways. This is because cooking is a bit of a novelty for them. Some wives complain that their husbands are a nightmare in the kitchen, using every vessel in the house including flowerpots and sick bowls as they follow their complicated, *MasterChef*-inspired recipes, but most of us are pleased at the joy it brings our menfolk and the opportunity it affords us to dust their clever books in peace while they're sequestered in the galley.

It's tempting to equate a husband's foodism with the 'hunter-gatherer instinct' but even anthropologists agree there's more to it than that. After all, some men never even boil an egg and they still come from good caveman stock. In fact, don't those chaps who refuse to try egg-boiling usually engage in a lot of typically manly stuff like bog-snorkelling and betting? Sure, everyone gets a buzz from providing for their family, but as it's still women who tend to do the daily fish-finger-slinging, and often grown-up supper too, cooking tends to be more of a special-occasion event for most married men. Sunday lunch, perhaps, or the legendary barbecue.

So many clichés about men are based on unkind false-hoods and generalisations, but the 'cooking meat outdoors' thing is just undeniably, gloriously true. On a recent camping trip with some other families, I woke at six a.m. (like many mothers of small children I am appar-ently 'a morning person'), got out my little gas stove to brew up some water for tea and then start making break-fast. The ignition switch on my rarely used stove wasn't working, though, so I called out, 'Anyone got a lighter? I can't get this thing to work.' Asleep only two seconds before, the men began to crawl and stumble towards me with the kind of determination and true, solemn kind-ness in their eyes that I have only seen in firemen and paramedics. I was quite moved. And I hadn't even got the sausages and big fork out yet. These modern-day heroes hadn't stopped to think, 'Who does have a lighter?' (turns out it was one of the other wives – the only one cool enough still to smoke), or even, 'Ah, she's probably just doing it wrong'; I was a human trying to harness fire to feed people in a field. And they were there for me.

The following morning, on the same trip, one of the husbands – a well-known late riser at the best of times – had been up half the night wrangling a crying child. When eight a.m. came around and people started thinking about bacon sandwiches, I fired up the stove again (with the help of my smoking buddy's Zippo), and called out, 'How many rashers shall I do?' One by one the slumbering menfolk rose, offering help, but I told them, 'No, it's OK, I've got this.' However, the exhausted late riser, who is also a great cook, a formidable eater and what I would call an extremely masculine and perfect man (gentle, brave, etc.) could not stay in bed and let someone else, male or female, attempt a fry-up. Every fibre of his being must have wanted to remain in that cosy sleeping bag, but something stronger than being-fibres propelled him up on to the sodden ground of a campsite at dawn to wrest the big fork from my hands and take charge of the grilling. I could see ancient things at work in him.

The interesting thing about the vibe on that camping trip (and there was a lot more man-tastic outdoor cooking crammed into that one weekend, including boiling things in a bucket on a stony beach and commandeering some scrap metal to rig up a makeshift grill behind someone's caravan) was that there was no suggestion from any of the men present that we women couldn't do the cooking properly. These were some enlightened dudes raised right by 1970s feminist mothers in scratchy polo necks: they know and love that women can do most things for themselves. Nor was it that they live emasculated, powerless urban lives: they were all ambitious, well-off men (all their own bosses, now I come to think of it), who gad around the globe doing daring and cool stuff. They swim in sharky oceans and even occasionally still do drugs! No, their desire to wield the outdoor frying pan came from somewhere deep within. I think the women present felt a version of it too, because we all got quite excited about the bedding situation and seeing how cosy we could make our kids at night. What cooking seemed to fulfil in these twenty-first-century husbands was something performative and social. If they were alone, surely they'd have just driven to the nearest café or begged a kettleful of water from the farmer's wife and made a Pot Noodle? But in the company of their fellow beings, it felt right to stand up and act.

I talked to the masculinity expert Justin Myers about this (he's not an academic but something better – a salacious columnist and witty novelist who has had to think more than most about his identity as a man because of pesky homophobes questioning his status all the time). He shared his take on the barbecuing phenomenon, born partly of being related to a brilliant outdoor chef of some renown who has honed his marinades and cooking times to perfection:

'It's a big performance of providing for people, but it's also a technique you have to master. A man has his speciality: he might try weird and interesting stuff. He knows the temperature, the timing, and it's all about perfecting it. It's a real project. It's hard to do well. And men like being successful in a challenge. He's got his big barbecuing sword – he's ready for battle!'

Even indoors, our attitudes to cooking seem inescapably gendered. As Myers says, 'All the major famous chefs are blokey, masculine men, and there's a lot of mythology behind that thing of "women are cooks, men are chefs" – there's extra respect given to a man who cooks.' And of course the antisocial working hours of cheffing certainly don't help bring women of childbearing age to the pass . . .

There's no doubt that women and men have different attitudes to cooking, just as we think differently about risk and communication and when to start Christmas shopping (which, come to think of it, is perhaps the ultimate manifestation of risk and communication). Our differences might be mostly socially constructed rather than to do with genetics. My go-to expert on such things, Tom Whipple, whose fascinating book on gender, *X and WHY*, is a must-read for every armchair pontificator, reckons it's often impossible to untangle the two. But many wives are secretly glad, nay awestruck, at their menfolk's warrior attitude to culinary mastery. For what woman would down tools in the middle of a long, painful Ottolenghi recipe to drive out to a Turkish deli for *labneh*? Who, after getting to that point three quarters of the way down an Elizabeth David recipe where she says 'add a dash of venison stock that's been reducing for six hours' would actually delay the meal until the next day and go out to get deer bones instead of saying, 'Fuck you, Elizabeth, your floor was so dirty you had to cover it with newspaper so you didn't fall over.'

Every woman I've talked to about following recipes says she usually tweaks it a bit, and maybe wouldn't bother measuring every single ingredient. I myself have never once followed every step of a recipe apart from when baking. Add 55 grams of minced onion to a mirepoix? Yeah right, I'm going to weigh my onion. I know what a mirepoix should look like. And I'm experienced, squeezed for time and I guess arrogant enough to believe that it doesn't matter if the ratio of allium to carrot is a bit off; that a dish will still turn out well if you use Greek yoghurt rather than strained Lebanese. But the truth is, everything my husband makes tastes better than my cooking, only I can't eat much of it because it's so rich. He puts chef-man-sized handfuls of salt in everything, and a whole pat of butter in most dishes. He does this because the men who write his favourite French recipes tell him to. Because it does taste good. And I suppose in restaurants they serve smaller portions than we do at home.

My definition of a successful recipe is something that ends with everyone feeling happy and the kitchen not looking like it's been sick down itself. It's something that children will eat, won't irritate anyone's latent IBS and won't stick to an earthenware dish (sorry gratins, you belong in a place with a paid pot-washer). Creating a well-judged dish that strikes the perfect balance between luxurious and fresh, thanks to hours of kitchen research by a professional man in a white coat who has stayed late in the restaurant kitchen again to perfect the recipes for his cookbook instead of going home and watching *Strictly* with his wife holds little appeal to me. Too much baggage in every bite.

After listening carefully to what husbands have to say about cooking, and reading lots of books by male chefs, I think Justin Myers is right: the husband in the kitchen is just fatally attracted to the science of it all.

Not to mention the completableness of it. Tom Whipple tells me that, in his house, he does all the cooking. 'I derive satisfaction from it because it's completable, unlike the Sisyphean task of daily housekeeping. I start – I make it – it looks good – it's finished – I get praised.'

And rightly. There was never a generation of such good-cooking husbands as there is now, and we are all the better fed for it. While wives might scoff at their menfolk for their slavish adherence to every detail of a recipe, we still all relish the results: good things cooked properly, with love.

The Husband Alone

'In solitude the mind gains strength and learns to lean upon itself.'

Laurence Sterne

'Have we got any crisps?'

SMS from husband ill at home to wife busy at work

It may surprise you to learn that David Beckham sometimes has a little cry in front of *Friends* when he's on his own.* My dad liked to take drugs. One erudite fiftysomething gent I know likes to get stuck into some online gambling when his wife is out. When we are all alone, with no one to judge or entertain us, our true selves can come out of hiding and do what feels right. So much of a husband's life is public these days – gone are the days of long weekend hours in his study, or epic Romantic rambles (which, as William Hazlitt, in his

* https://www.gq.com/story/david-beckham-cover-protecting-kids-brooklyn

lovely essay 'On Going a Journey', reminds us, are best done alone). The modern husband's leisure hours must be spent accompanying friends and family on the many pointless and expensive missions that make up modern life, which usually involve queuing, parking, yelling and wondering if you're wearing the wrong shoes.

When I ask men what they do when they are home alone, I always say 'apart from the obvious', by which I mean pleasures of the flesh but which most seem to interpret as 'stuff that smells'. Because very many of the men I've spoken to about their one-on-none time say that the first thing they do when the door closes (or slams, depending on how things are) behind their exiting partner is not to think, 'Right, time to fire up that website I accidentally found accidentally the other day' but, 'I'm going to fry me a damn fish!'

Kitchen pongs are a real point of contention between husbands and wives. So much so that one wonders whether all those studies which rate 'sex and money' as the main sources of conflict in a relationship don't mention 'shallow-frying whitebait' only because it's so obvious it goes without saying.

There may, for once, be some hard science to explain matters here, because biology boffins agree that women tend to have a keener sense of smell than men.* It's all about a cute-sounding region of the brain called the olfactory bulb. Women have more brain cells in it, and

* https://www.medicalnewstoday.com/articles/284991.php

so in general are better able to perceive aromas of all kinds. And as many women know, pregnancy causes this clever talent for smelling stuff to skyrocket, making the world an intolerable place to be for several months of her confinement.

Pregnancy aside, most husbands will hear the phrase, 'What's that smell?' almost as frequently in their married life as the phrase, 'Well it doesn't sound any different to me' when they are showing their wife a new way of listening to music. And, to be fair to all the ladies out there who frequently have to raise a handkerchief or item of clothing to their noses (ever wondered why polo necks and high collars have been consistently on-trend in mum-fashion for the last hundred years?), it's not just a subtle way of objectifying men as primal ogres. Chaps simply do more pungent stuff than women: terrible beery horse-pees, sweats from lifting too-heavy weights and gas proudly released straight into the air of communal spaces. And triumphant burps. Marriage was basically invented to police these foul odours.

'My wife doesn't really like fish,' my mate Neil tells me, 'so when she's out that's one of the things I like to do. That and play my guitar,' which presumably she hates too.

For another man of my acquaintance, it's hot wings. His wife, he reasons, could be expected to tolerate the smoky miasma of deep-frying chicken scraps, and even the death-defying whole pat of melted butter with which he will joyously coat meat, kitchen and self. But add to the mix, as he must, two bottles of astringent Franks Hot Sauce and the whole scene transcends anything promised in the marriage vows. This considerate fellow sometimes does his wife the favour of sleeping apart from her on Wing Night, too, since a snack that intestinally corrosive just keeps on giving.

Nasty-smelling food that gives you wind and kills you is obviously vitally important to many men, and is generally accepted by their wives – in reasonable doses – along with their need for shouting at the telly, crying over baby photos and truly believing that they could run the country better than the prime minister as just one of the sustaining habits that keeps the modern husband comfortable in his own skin. But there's something else they do when they're alone that many partners are less keen to condone, and that is the consumption of terrible media. What do you do when your wife's out, Jim? I innocently ask.

'Watch box sets or films she doesn't like.'

'You mean blokey sci-fi stuff like *The Lord of the Rings*?'

'No, dark material.'

And he's not talking about the popular Philip Pullman novels. It's those gory killing pageants so beloved of today's viewer that float his boat.

Another friend, a peaceful, indeed hippyish guy whose wife is a tough lady but doesn't relish a night in, munching popcorn, to the soundtrack of visceral murder and sexually motivated violence, also waits until she goes out to get stuck into that sort of television drama that always peaks with a sweaty, half-naked woman yelping in fear.

Why do sweet, kind men (women too but I'm not friends with them) love this stuff? Is it because their animal brains need exposure to nature red in tooth and claw? Is it an antidote to the super-safe physical environment they live in? Do they need to replay the worst thing that can happen to make it a bit less scary? Are they disgusting murder-beasts pretending to be normal people?

Either way, I guarantee that, right now, there are thousands if not millions of home-alone husbands watching the grimmest things to ever pass the censors. So don't come home early . . .

Unless of course you want to find your man doing the one thing that is more annoying and offensive than anything else. After much pressing on my part, a busy local dad I know confessed that the one thing he loves to do when his wife is out is 'nothing. Chilling, relaxing.' With all the pressures of modern family life which, remember, now require men to do things other than having a nice sit-down after work, this is the ultimate taboo activity: idleness. Like every serious social researcher, I assume that most men are telling only partial truths when I interview them about their habits, but as I can't imagine anything more vexing to a wife than her husband sitting on the sofa staring happily into space all day, I actually believe that this is the whole truth and nothing but.

Some men do things that are quite disgusting when their wives go out, and I'm still not talking about 'the obvious'.

'What do you get up to when the missus is out?' I asked an old friend.

'Grooming,' he whispered furtively. To most women, me included, this sounds like a sufficiently innocent activity not to require isolation. But according to this confessor, few ladies have ever seen a man really grooming himself, because it's not what you think it's going to be. It involves blades, medicated swabs, bicarb and small bowls of vinegar and needs to be done over a towel with a torch between the teeth. Remember that scene in the post-kids comedy film, *This is Forty*, where Hollywood heart-throb Paul Rudd lies on his back with a mirror angled south, legs akimbo, drawers off but black work socks on, and says to his wife, 'I need you to look at something'? It's like that. But worse. And with a DIY guide to minor surgery playing on YouTube.

Husbands and Their Friends

''Tis the privilege of friendship to talk nonsense, and to have her nonsense respected.'

Charles Lamb

The idea for this book grew out of a conversation between me and my husband about how we talk to our friends. Specifically, how often we mention our private parts in one phone conversation. For women, there's nothing more bonding and relaxing than describing the exact proportion of crêpey skin to cellulite on your inner thighs, or what you reckon a man's nether regions might look like at seventy, and this doesn't change when you get married. In fact, it probably intensifies, given all the horrible things that happen to your body after the age of thirty. We women live for this stuff. We love it because it's more fascinating and funny than talking about mortgages and schools, and it reminds us that we've got each other's (acne-scarred, sweaty, fat) backs.

Time and time again, women report asking their husbands, 'So what did you talk about?' after he returns from a night out with friends. Friends who presumably, being human, are all in the throes of various romantic dramas, health crises and existential wobbles. You know the answer: 'Nothing.' If pushed – like if they've actually been on a four-day stag party or a funeral or something – they might say, 'You know. Stuff.' One thing they will absolutely never ever ever talk about is whether any of them are having affairs. I have this on good authority from a man in his sixties with oodles of close and naughty friends who basically does nothing but have long lunches and go for drinks. He says that an admission of infidelity would be unthinkable. Why? 'It's private.'

I used to think men were all lying about their boring chat and that actually as soon as they were out of earshot of their wives, they were all, 'OMG one of her boobs is legit getting bigger than the other, lolz', but that really doesn't seem to be the case. Married men are coy. They are proper. They really do like talking about sport and politics. Having been butt-dialled on numerous occasions by drunken chaps in my social circle, I can attest to the extreme uninterestingess of most gent-on-gent chat. Husbands really do not reveal intimate secrets to their mates at great length and in disgusting detail over their craft beers and technical coffees. Why? Partly because it would be shameful and embarrassing but mostly because instead of making them feel all close and conspiratorial, it could make things awkward: 'I wouldn't want to burden them with my problems,' one friend said, before telling me how grateful he is to have his wife to unburden himself on. This is all very alien to women, I must say.

Occasionally, however, a man will admit to talking about something verging on human interest with his cronies, and it's nearly always while busily engaged in a practical activity. (Tip: this is also a good way to get children to open up. At least those who don't respond well to being dragged away from their toys, stared at intensely and asked, '*Is there anything you want to talk to me about?*')

Ben, a feelings-friendly American, is one such 'kinetic talker' (another American, a colleague, used this phrase in all seriousness when suggesting we go for a walk instead of having our meeting in an office). For him, opening up involves hiking boots and a daysack:

'My guy friends and I do talk about fairly intimate things, including relationship stuff. I just got back from the camping trip I do every summer with some other male friends, and we spent a lot of time talking about having kids, what marital sex lives are like, trying to be supportive of wives in career crisis, etc. We also talked a lot about farting and *Star Wars*. So it's a mix. But the mix has definitely changed in proportion over the years. In fact, I remember vividly that when we were heading out on our first trip eight years ago, one of us was freaking out because his wife was unexpectedly pregnant with their first kid. Three of the five of us were single, no one had kids, and no one really knew what to say. Eight years later, everyone's married and leaning heavily into life as a middle-aged husband, and in the next two years or so everyone will probably have kids. It's been really special to go through that change of seasons together. And our banter on the trail has changed with our stages of life.'

How I love these men! And how lucky are their wives to have husbands with this natural, regular release-valve for the issues that could build up inside them, which doesn't involve doing something stupid and dangerous and is cheaper than therapy.

Ben's free-flowing guy-talk would horrify most Englishmen, especially those of a certain age.

Frank, a veteran of the local pub-quiz scene where I live, and a man who – despite looking like a 1930s duke – has many female friends and is quite a chatterbox and not at all uptight, added a striking vignette to the mystery surrounding husbands and their friends. He has been meeting up with a group of married, male colleagues for lunch every month for a number of years. It's purely a social thing – a treat involving lots of food and booze, and a long afternoon chatting and relaxing. But through-out all their many years of get-togethers, no one had ever mentioned his sex life. In the last year, though, all of a sudden, this naughtiest of subjects has begun to be broached. 'How exciting!' I said, assuming that the floodgates having opened, they were all drawing cartoon dicks on their napkins and dealing little blue pills under the table by the time the pudding trolley came round (I think we can assume there was a pudding trolley). But no. The sex talk was described as brief, awkward and very non-specific. No visceral descriptions? No re-enactments using carrots and blobs of mash? My gentlemanly companion winced. God no.

Which is not to say that husbands don't get love and support from their friends equal to what their wives can offer. It's just harder to understand. Because it doesn't look like love; more like repressed, not very friendly banter.

When a husband goes on a lads' holiday to Estonia and comes back looking ill, smelling weird and reporting that 'nothing' was talked about, he is not necessarily lying. This should comfort any fretful brides-to-be who have watched the *Hangover* movies and are covertly examining their fiancés for monkey bites while they sleep. He probably just has different friends for different things. One chap told me that if something really difficult was happening in his life, he'd rather pay to see a therapist than offload his woes on to his friends. The fear that opening up to other men could tarnish the fun escapism of your time together is a major issue for many men, who, like Frank's lunch club, sometimes take years to get comfortable enough together to feel they can risk intimacy.

Of course, it's hard for women to relate to this, as most of our friendships tend to be flexible enough to cry together one minute and holler mindlessly at the telly the next. But several men I've spoken to have clear ideas of which friends are good for what.

In one male friendship group I know, there's one bloke who famously will never talk about emotional stuff and is useless for personal advice sessions, but a couple of others who will openly weep and wail and rage together like members of a Burning Man rebirthing circle. When two members of this group talked independently to me about no-feelings Norman, I couldn't help feeling a bit worried about him and his silence, wondering if something in his past had made him shut down. But then it occurred to me that he probably just has a different group of mates for his personal chats. Maybe he thinks the tearful twosome are sadly misguided in their post-Lacanian approach to the subconscious, and he'd rather throw in his lot with some more traditional Freudians who understand that many classic theories of the mind can be helpfully reframed for the contemporary male experience in a more rational and considered way. It's most likely that.

I do know husbands of a certain age who have very sentimental friendships, usually based on shared past experience, and there's something supremely sweet and gallant about these pairings. After all, old friends start to matter a great deal as we get older and move away from the harbour of our early lives into the uncharted waters of marriage, where many men are a little apathetic when it comes to making new friends and will happily let their wives take over arranging their new joint social lives. Arranging outings and dinner parties and concert tickets seems to be another example of a 'skill' that women 'just seem better at', like wiping up spills and icing biscuits.

Perhaps it's a talent honed in the years of being at home with babies and arranging to see other mothers so they don't go mad; or it may come from our ability to put ourselves out there and say to other humans, 'I like you and I want to see you', which is a step too vulnerable for many a husband. But of course, men love camaraderie and social hi-jinks as much as anyone. Chaps who as little boys were forced to share a bedroom on a school trip or family holiday might have grumbled about it at the time, but will reminisce bromantically over those midnight snacks and memorable farts decades later, like old veterans who can only understand each other. This often comes across in best-man speeches which, if you strip away the dirty jokes and insincere compliments, are really a very moving love letter from one young knight to another. In fact, they can be quite traumatic if the groom and best man are true besties, since it marks the first and last time they can openly profess their love for one another.

The sociologist Niobe Way, co-director of the Center for Research on Culture, Development, and Education at New York University, has observed that when boys are prepubescent, they will speak about their male best friend in explicitly loving terms, acknowledging and naming their bond as special, emotional and almost miraculous. By the age of sixteen, however, that has all shut down, and however much they love their friends, their anxiety about seeming gay will always trump their desire to express admiration or, worse, need for another male.

Although the terror of appearing homosexual lessens over time for most men – be they gay or straight – it seems that they rarely regain their ability to say those three little words to their friends. 'I love you, man' has become a comedic trope and the title of an ironic, gawky bromance movie. In real life, it's something men say only when they're blackout drunk or in terrible trouble.

Which is a shame, because they will tell their wives that they love their male friends till the cows come home and get quite misty-eyed about it. Could it be that they hope (subconsciously or otherwise) that their wives will pass on their message of love to their friends' wives and so to the friends themselves, like mummies helping their little ones establish friendships at nursery, so they don't have to do the risky work themselves?

Husbands in the Workplace

Shh! Don't Wake Dad!

Cruising the aisles of a toyshop with my children as a reward for having spent five minutes in a museum, I came across a board game called, Shh! Don't Wake Dad! It's one of the new generation of batteries-not-included board games in which the fun of winning is enhanced by noise and moving parts. The aim of this one is to creep round a board showing a rudimentary floor-plan of a house without setting off any of the little sounds – a hooting owl, a howling cat – which might do the terrible, horrible deed of *waking Dad*. Dad, a little plastic man in a little plastic bed in the centre of the board, will then sit up in bed raging angrily or, if you're lucky, bemusedly, against whatever has interrupted his slumber.

It's evidently a popular game, judging by the fact that it's been around for years and the scores of under-tens who have come to our house to play it (because of course I bought it) find it unfailingly amazing. Clearly it taps in to a major truth about husbands and fathers: the idea that – because what they do when they're awake is so important and tough – they must be allowed to get their sleep.

Now, this is a tricky phenomenon to unpick because, in many households, when the children are small, it is indeed true that without the husband being relied upon to go to work and earn money, the pantry would be bare. So if he is kept up all night comforting babies, or is disturbed in his little plastic bed at five a.m. by noisy cats, it could be a real problem. Especially if he does a job where it's not OK to fall asleep at work, like surgery or driving a bus.

The 'natural', as we used to see it, role of the wife is to stay at home shagging the milkman and breastfeeding, while it behoves a man to go out into the world and follow his career dreams or at least bring home some money. Even though nowadays many women choose or have to return to work when their babies are still small, and leave it to nannies and grannies to shag the milkman all day, the notion that a husband's job is more important persists. It's a deeply held idea that has led to the gender pay gap, where women are under-represented in high-paid, executive positions because those jobs are incompatible with the wife's massively time-consuming unpaid second job of being the main housekeeper and child-carer.

When we do find a hugely successful woman, a CEO, say, or a prime minister, she is usually full of praise for her wonderful husband who helps take care of their ten children or at least does the 'Boy's Job' of taking the bins out. But the notion persists, in most families, that the husband's work is more important, and when we look at the way his working life is set up, it's a wonder that any marriage can survive a husband's extramarital love-affair with the workplace. It's not that most men adore what they do; it's just such a big part of their life that it becomes a real force in their emotional and mental lives. A bit like a lover, or a really needy, annoying friend. It reinforces their status as useful and powerful in a way that family life alone can't. This is shady territory, though, because many millions of women get all their confidence from their careers and absolutely hate to be seen primarily as a mother and wife. Similarly, I know a house-husband or two, currently at home with small children while the wife goes out to work who, if it weren't for the constraints of living on a single income, would happily never go to the office again. Because once you really get into it, there are so many ways to shine and grow as a man at home. And so many women around between nine and five to admire you for it.

'The pressures of work and travel' are often given as reasons for celeb love-rifts, and while it seems a bit much to be complaining that flying around the world in a private jet could make you want to dump your partner, these constraints are real problems in real marriages:

First, there's the daily commute (not to mention longer business trips). An hour in the car or on the train each morning puts the husband on a metaphorical and actual fast-track out of hearth and home. By the time he gets into the office, the bloom of the marriage bed (or spare room) has worn off, and he has morphed into the man he is between nine and five. And that's a man who doesn't stop to call his wife ten times a day 'just because' (or just because she's having a terrible time and needs his support); a man who must engage in banter about stuff he doesn't really care about and eat and drink when he doesn't fancy it. He may have more or less power over his co-workers than he does over the other residents of his house. And because he spends so much time in this non-dom environment, it's no wonder it starts to define him and exert an irresistible pull on him. Relationships at work are intense, especially if travel, teamwork on special projects and social networking are a part of it.

You can even buy novelty mugs for in-office tea drinking that say 'work wife' and 'work hubby' on them. And they're from John Lewis, bastion of family values.

Going to work doesn't just give a husband a taste of a different identity: it fulfils his desire to provide for his family. Work is what he does to play his role as a married man properly. And with all this going on, it's no surprise that sometimes the old testosterone and brain start messaging each other a bit too much and get confused: is it manly to love work so much that you shag your secretary? Errr . . .

Let's look at some real-life examples from what strikes me to be the worst job in the world: the politician.

I once shared a taxi back from a party with a man who worked in Parliament. It was five a.m. and it had been a long night of men shouting about politics and showcasing various alpha-ish postures and practices. As dawn broke over the Thames, my seat-mate's mobile rang. From his attempts to sound sober and caring, I gathered it was his wife. After a few apologies, he said, 'But your waters haven't actually broken though, right?' I wondered, for a moment, whether contrary to all I'd heard about him being a loving family man, he was in fact the world's worst husband. Then I realised he'd just got confused about who his real family was: which House was his home?

I saw this phenomenon up close when I spent six months with a US election campaign. Here were dozens of people of all ages who had put their lives on hold to try to get their chosen candidate elected. They'd left family, friends and jobs to rent crappy apartments and stay up all night manning the phones and writing sound bites in the hope of changing the world. They went on trips together and drank in local bars after work. It was intense. It was very much like a family. Unwise affairs were conducted, and intimate friendships formed that still stand strong twenty years later. Like a film set, the bubble of that campaign became a family to everyone involved. And afterwards, when the dust had settled on the candidate's failed bid and everyone went back to where they came from, there were many painful losses.

This experience gave me an insight into why politicians keep having silly affairs. You might think it's all about power, and in the classic MP/PA dalliance that's surely a major factor. But there's something else at play too, and that's the precious feeling of being understood and accepted as in the ideal family; the family we might think we remember from our youth, and are compelled to reimagine. With political jobs taking people away from their spouses and children so often, it's no surprise if the house containing the resentful, lonely wife and distant kids starts to feel less like a supportive home than the office, where those late hours and short-notice trips are not only accepted but praised as a badge of honour. Add into the mix the 'higher calling' of saving the world, and the quotidian round of nappies and ironing seems a bit pointless. And much to the annoyance of many wives, pretty much any job can be made to look like a vital cog in the world's ability to turn if you spin it right.

I asked a Westminster veteran if my suspicions were right about all this:

'The nights are not as late as they were, and there is very little drinking nowadays. But I think you are right that the political vortex replaces other relationships. Being down at Westminster – and particularly being at party conferences – is comparable to being on a cricket tour. You are away from home, you eat at canteens and restaurants, usually with someone, you rarely have much silence, you are living out of a suitcase and every day brings its variety of bouncers and cow-shots and dicey decisions by the umpire. Blokes quite like cricket tours, but when they get home after one they feel knackered and they also feel a sense of anticlimax which is quickly picked up on by their wives, who proceed to shout at them or roll into a hedgehog ball until the man is prepared to be more civilised.'

I also spoke to a former White House staffer about the phenomenon:

'The work was so intense that office life did naturally expand to encompass one's social life and romantic life, too. It's a very ensconcing world, and everyone in it is going through the same intense thing together, and that creates a kind of social momentum ... to the point where you feel like work life is your "real" life and what's actually important. And I think a lot of relationships suffer because of that.'

And when the political husband does finally return to his real home – what then? Is it a struggle to get back into doing the washing-up after dealing with lofty affairs of state? My Westminster chum relates:

'The wise politico will throw himself into domestic chores for two reasons: it establishes a pax with the memsahib and it keeps him sane, or at least less mad. I usually find, when I get home on a Thursday, that the fridge is empty, the kitchen is a mess and the dogs' kennel needs cleaning. It takes me about two hours to "decompress" – i.e. to change mind gears, after doing the post, going shopping, tidying up, etc. – when I get back home at the end of the political week.'

Much has been written about political marriages, and the intersection between a public figure's duty to their People versus their people. The ones that look most successful seem to be between couples like Clementine and Winston Churchill or Margaret and Denis Thatcher, or Jacinda Ardern and that pretty fisherman, where one person plays a supporting role to their powerful spouse, allowing them to devote their energies to their job without demanding a full-time partner and co-parent too. But what makes a marriage successful, really? I heard one historian say that Churchill, although a cheeky boy who loved the ladies, was able to stay away from real scandal because he was not by nature a sexual predator. And who knows what the Thatchers' marriage really felt like on the inside?

What's certain is that public life isn't easy. Charles and Diana, Caesar and Calpurnia ... and who knows whether the marriage of Donald and Melania Trump isn't in fact the mutually invigorating, respectful union it appears to be?

The reason we all jump on gossip about, say, David and Victoria Beckham's marriage is because schadenfreude and anxiety about our own lives can be played out perfectly on the global celeb stage. What would we do if our husband was the most gorgeous man alive and everyone wanted him? Could we keep him? Where would we send our kids to school if money were no object but we wanted them to stay 'grounded'? What would we wear if we were that thin? Would we smile? These are questions about ourselves, not Mrs Beckham.

It's a kind of auto-therapy, looking at famous marriages weather the storms of celebrity life. Brad and Angelina:

too many kids? Madonna and Guy: too many weird hats?

Then what happens if the woman becomes more famous than the man? Can a marriage survive such a radical power imbalance? There was speculation that Lady Diana's celebrity annoyed her husband. Could our own relationship survive a shift like that?

Supreme Court superhero Ruth Bader Ginsburg and her late husband Martin have become folk heroes of modern, feminist marriage, and there's a good reason why. It's this kind of couple – not Posh & Becks – that we should look to for inspiration. Martin had his own career as a lawyer but came to relish the work of supporting his wife in her groundbreaking role as well. He is still remembered for baking cakes for her clerks' birthdays and generally being an all-round paragon of husbandism, without whom America's most important female law-maker would have had a much harder time combining work and family.

It's important to note that theirs was no unequal partnership, where he stayed at home darning her lace jabots while she stayed up late smoking cigars in clubs. There were times, such as when Martin was ill shortly after their first child was born in the 1950s, that Ruth became his nurse as well as raising a newborn, attending both their classes and taking his dictated notes, as well as producing the *Harvard Law Review*. Later on, as RBG told the interviewer Rachel Maddow, there were times when Martin took over at home: 'In the course of a marriage, one accommodates the other. So, for example, when Marty was intent on becoming a partner in a New York law firm in five years, during that time, I was the major caretaker of our home and child. But when I started up the ACLU Women's Rights Project, Marty realized how important that work was.'*

Research shows that pay equality and shared domestic duties make for happier marriages, and this goes for all people in all kinds of jobs, not only top American lawyers. If a husband has a traditional office job and the wife, like many, works part time, it's easy to fall into the old pattern of the husband coming home at seven and putting his feet up. It's understandable that a man earning thousands of pounds a week and giving it all to his family might feel entitled to certain treats when he's not at the office. But he'll be missing out on the biggest treat of all – a mutually supportive, fun, involved and fulfilling marriage – if he lets his frazzled wife do all the laundry, all the washing-up and plan all the nights out.

The Ginsburgs manifested the joy of a truly equal partnership for decades, until Martin's passing in 2010. In the 2015 biography *The Notorious RBG: The Life and Times of Ruth Bader Ginsburg*, the couple's daughter spoke about the last days of her father: 'If my first memories are of Daddy cooking, so are my last.

---

* https://mic.com/articles/110848/9-quotes-prove-ruth-bader-ginsburg-has-all-the-relationship-advice-you-ll-ever-need#.RaAN7dg3f

Cooking for Mother even when he could not himself eat, nor stand in the kitchen without pain, because for him it was ever a joy to discuss the law over dinner with Mother while ensuring that she ate well and with pleasure.'*

* https://jezebel.com/marty-was-always-my-best-friend-ruth-bader-gins-burgs-l-1738733789

Husbands and Pets

'It's tough to stay married. My wife kisses the dog on the
lips, yet she won't drink from my glass.'

Rodney Dangerfield

A chance remark by a friend about the role his dog
played in their family life led me to ask the internet
about pets and marriage. The first thing that came up
was 'Can you legally marry a dog?'. Which is why proper
writers do research in the British Library first, and on
Google never. But then, they might miss important
details about the real, insane love that real, insane people
have for their animals and how it impacts their human
affairs.

In *Kudos*, Rachel Cusk's brilliant, sort-of-true novel
about middle-aged ennui, we meet a man who has made
a right hash of family life and marriage by working away
too much and drifting apart from his wife and children.
He is left to care for their beloved old dog while the rest
of the household are away. But on his watch, the dog
appears to go into a morbid decline and he makes the

decision to have it put down. It's hard but he wants to do the right thing: the unemotional, kind, manly thing. He must show leadership and tough kindness, like a proper father. So the vet comes and administers the fatal dose. Then Bad Dad has to bury that big, furry, doggy body that his children had loved so much. And oh, the fall-out when his wife and kids discover what he's done! You don't have to be a literary genius like Cusk to show us what this means: we play out our unresolved internal dramas on our pets, who are usually easier to interact with than other humans.

Sometimes a man's dog is not his best friend, and that can cause problems too. The chance remark that set me thinking about all this was from a long-married friend, Morgan, whose wife did the usual and perfectly natural thing of getting a wolfhound puppy when their four kids were too big to carry around and tickle behind the ears. Rex (are dogs still called Rex?; in my local park, calling that name out in a game of Dog or Sprog would probably see more humans than canines come running) was a big hit. With the wife and children and all the neighbouring wives and children anyway: an adorable pup whose floppy ears and perfect snout were cartoon-cute. He was well trained, loyal and loving. But daddy just wasn't feeling it. He didn't hate the dog; he just didn't actually love it. Didn't miss it when they went away on holiday; didn't blithely clear up its horrid messes with an indulgent smile. And this lack of emotional investment became a juicy bone of contention with the missus.

She began to ask him why he didn't love the dog more; why he didn't give it more attention. Maybe he should spend more time alone with Rex, she suggested? Was there something in his past that made it hard for him to get close to dogs?! What's wrong with you!

All this emotive analysis was confusing to my friend: he liked Rex well enough – he just wasn't completely obsessed with him like everyone else seemed to be. And in fact he wouldn't mind getting a bit more of that sort of attention himself . . .

Like in Cusk's story, this is when a dog means a whole lot more than a dog. It has become – in fact it is deliberately made into – the repository of everyone's unspoken desires. Isn't that why a man gets a dog in the first place? To be his best friend? To give him the kind of explicit, spoken (well, woofed) affirmation of love that his two-legged mates can't?

One of my neighbours keeps tropical fish. I've met a few chaps like this over the years: burly, hard-working men who like fixing and lifting stuff and whose wives keep lovely, neat homes. In fact, I can recall three households where fish were evidently at the sentimental centre of the husband's life. In each of these traditional domestic set-ups, the stay-at-home mum kept everything immaculate, ironing socks and dusting the Lego, while the husband worked out of the home and got his work clothes ripped off him for laundering and probably other things when he came in. These affectionate and loving dudes were top dads, spending the evenings playing with their sons and daughters and helping with homework. They ate dinner together as a family and, afterwards, the husband enjoyed drinks and flirty chats with his pretty wife who always had her nails done. Good times. But these men had a secret obsession. The fish tank. When they were alone, or their families were busy, they would sit for hours watching their sparkly little minnows go about their fishy family lives. They might tinker with the filter, recheck the oxygen levels, scrupulously dismantle and clean every part of the aquarium's apparatus. Even wash the gravel, which is the equivalent of ironing socks and dusting Lego. Instead of (OK, maybe as well as) looking at gentleman's websites, they spent their evenings engrossed in magazines and blogs about the latest bits of aquatic kit and breeds of fish.

This obsessive behaviour will be familiar to husband-watchers everywhere, as it has all the characteristics of what grown men seem to like best: a complex mechanical toy; a system with very specific instructions and predictable outcomes; and a collection to complete. But when it comes to animal husbandry, there's more to it than that. The fish-daddy is deep into monitoring his creatures' behaviour and wellbeing too. He seems really to love them. He will carefully section off any fish that might be pregnant or aggressive, keeping an eye out for the little ones, checking for any that might be showing signs of stress.

Here is a way for a man to wrest back some control over the domestic sphere that his wife dominates, and all under the guise of a technical, practical hobby. To succeed at the ultimate fatherly act of providing for every physical and emotional need of his brood, from food to shelter to helping manage conflict. And hey, if there's a bit of collecting and engineering involved, so much the better. When things go wrong, such as when all the baby fish get eaten, which is apparently quite common, it plays out in front of the husband's eyes as if he's having a bad dream or watching a gruesome murder show on TV: the worst you can imagine being acted out safely, framed in miniature for you to watch. It doesn't hurt you, and you can turn away from it, perhaps a little desensitised. Who knows what trauma, real or imagined, is being worked through when a man tinkers with his fish tank.

Families have more to thank their pets for than they realise. I know a pukka old gent who has little threadbare patches on the left arm of all his jerseys where his beloved puss habitually pads him with its claws when they cuddle because he is kitty's mummy. He refuses his wife's darning needle and wears those jumpers with pride. And it's as adorable as those little patches of regurgitated milk on the shoulder of a new mother's dress because it's a messy little symbol of nurture and love. Animals do so much emotional work for us: we all know the trope of the sad or disenfranchised child bonding with a pet where human contact can't reach her. We see the comfort a dog brings to someone living on the streets or suffering the loneliness of advanced old age.

These are scenes that lend themselves to inspirational internet clips with schmaltzy music, but the less meme-worthy image of a big man reading a tropical fish magazine late at night is, to me, equally powerful. So think twice before teasing a man about his wormery, his terrarium or his bath full of newts. Apart from those weirdos who keep massive snakes in the spare room. Stay away from them.

Husbands Who Jump into Rivers (and run around in Lycra)

'Bid me run, and I will strive with things impossible.'
William Shakespeare, *Julius Caesar*

Sport, from darts to fives to cheese-rolling, has long been the most popular means for a husband to escape his wife and children. It's a culturally sanctioned alternative to the shopping-childcare-talking-to-the-woman-you-married nexus of the modern man's downtime that few wives forbid, since it puts a chap in a good mood and keeps him out of the pub. Apart from darts.

But physical activity – the more extreme the better – has taken over from all other passions including betting and shouting at the telly as the recreation of choice for the modern husband. Thanks to vanity, smart technology and the desire not to die, parks and lakes in cities all over the globe are positively bulging with sweaty men in funny outfits being bossed around by their watches on Saturday and Sunday mornings.

Like twenty-first-century Lord Byrons leaping into the Grand (Union) Canal, men are casting off their work-aday slacks and taking to open water by the thousands. Triathlon is the new everything. Parkruns, swimruns, charity 5ks ... these are now in the ordinary lexicon of the modern husband and his bemused wife, who, even if she herself can outrun a gazelle and bench-press 100 pounds, is typically left to hold the fort at home while the 'athlete' in the family travels hundreds of miles to an important weekend 'meet'. The lure of Day-Glo, sweat-wicking Edwardian bathing suits and the chance to exert themselves until they are sick and feeling awesome is as compelling as putting ten bob on the horses once was. It's tribal. It's addictive. And I want to know why so many of my friends have lost their husbands to it.

For the uninitiated, endurance sport is a lot to get your head round. Why take part in something painful where you'll never be a nice temperature? Why the funny clothes? It's something I've thought and read about quite a lot because I've long been fascinated by ultra-running, big-wall rock climbing, and in fact all extreme endur-ance sports. It's my absolutely favourite thing to do vicariously when quadruple-insulated in my bed with pyjamas, duvet, hot-water bottle and cat. I have tried rock climbing and yes it's amazing, but only about the same amazingness as staying home reading about it, and staying home has the advantage of not worrying some-one is looking up at your bum from a funny angle when you're reaching for a hold, or that you're about to die.

Also, climbers don't talk much while they're climbing, which is a shame because some of the world's best climbers and runners (and maybe cyclists, but I'm too freaked out by their horrid shoes to read books by them) also turn out to be brilliant prose stylists; perhaps not surprising given the creativity and open-mindedness needed to summit El Cap with nothing but a carrot to eat and a bag to poo in. And they sure do present a fascinating study of modern masculinity.

Here are men who leave the comforts of the marital bed to put themselves through extreme physical and mental hardship in a usually all-male environment because if they didn't do it they wouldn't be able to enjoy (tolerate?) the softness of twenty-first-century living.

This idea is certainly borne out by the men where I live, who – whether bankers or bus drivers – seem to all be completely obsessed with pushing their plucky dad-bods as far as they will go, making Hampstead Heath at the weekend look like a charity fun-run for a very specific, Lycra-loving subsection of the bear and otter community.

Endurance sport has never been more popular in the UK, and it's men leading the charge. A quarter of a million people applied to run the London marathon last year, the majority of them men. Since the 2012 Olympics, membership of British Cycling has increased from 45,000 to 100,000. Swimming in urban lakes has taken off too, with events such as Swim Serpentine in London, and it's thought there are 140,000 'active triathletes' in the UK.* Yes, women do this stuff in increasing numbers too, and are amazing at it, but the majority of those shrink-wrapped bottoms you stand behind trying to ignore when queuing up to get your Sunday morning coffee are male.

One of them lives in my road. He is a semi-pro swim-runner, as far as I can tell from the fact that he often wears Lycra and has his arm in a sling. He also looks as clear-skinned and bright-eyed as an actual baby. A very lean, fit baby with a big watch. I know he travels the world to compete in events, and thinks nothing of knocking out a quick marathon before lunch. So I asked him what he thinks of the growing trend amongst men for speeding about the place in Lycra:

'My view is that these are almost 100 per cent analogue experiences, so give us a break from our digital lives. Plus a lot of the added growth in running and cycling also has to do with the social element. Swimrun is an example: people love the total immersion in nature and, crucially, you are racing with a mate. It's a tribe, through and through.'

Put like that, it's hard to see why any modern man would not give it a try. After all, digital culture and loneliness are today's top indicators for mental stress, and although there must be nothing worse for a depressed

* https://www.sports-insight.co.uk/trends-features/more-people-are-taking-part-in-endurance-sport-than-ever-before

person than some perky jogger saying 'Try going for a run!', it's hard to see how joining a supportive tribe of serotonin-fuelled outdoorsmen could make you feel worse. Plus it'll make you look good too, and help counteract the early warning signs of old age, as my (apparently ageless – forty? sixty?) neighbour points out:

'There's also the realisation that you need to be proactive with your health, i.e. eating well is often not enough. To de-stress, lose weight and have fun, sport must feature in the mix.'

But it's not just sport, is it? We're not talking about a chummy football game in the park. These are activities that can make you bleed and puke and break bones. Do these otherwise cosseted chaps – whisper it – actually like the pain?

'The odd thing is, embracing pain is key to a greater performance and therefore overall enjoyment. You know the pain is coming, but there's no fear attached to it. On the contrary.'

Far out. And isn't handling pain a big part of what it means to be a man? We decry the culture of 'manning up' and 'boys don't cry', but isn't it rather brilliant for any human to learn not to fear pain? Could it be that the 'man-up' brigade (as well as being a street gang of North London public-school boys) actually have their hearts in the right place and are aiming for a true path through life as impervious to external irritants as the actual Buddha? My sporty neighbour certainly seems pretty chilled.

So what, I ask him, apart from the small matter of spiritual enlightenment, is the ultimate aim of all this matey masochism? Increased life expectancy? A rocking body? Getting out of the house in a way that makes it unlikely your wife will follow you?

'There are many things at play here – a healthy life in soul and body is a great by-product for me (but many super-fit athletes do suffer from mental issues). There is also – as with work – some benefit in showing your children that things don't just fall in your lap. That there's nothing that prevents you from venturing outside your comfort zone; and usually when you do so the rewards can be surprisingly high.'

Go daddy!

The idols for people like my neighbour are guys like Scott Jurek, the vegan long-distance runner, or that Dutch bloke who hyperventilates and sits in ice baths to boost his immune system. It seems that a big part of honing your body is to avoid ending up dead at fifty. It's also about vanity of course (which is sort of the same thing, death not being such a great look), and that peculiarly male desire to adhere to a set of instructions which will result in a predictable outcome.

One happily married friend, a top academic with a nice, stable home life, identified in himself a desire to do something a bit fast and thrilling, so conducted a detailed risk-reward comparison of various types of sport from surfing to stock-car racing. He lighted on a particular kind of motor racing. But in order to probably not be killed, he figured out that you should only do it on certain days and times, when the most likely causers of accidents (aggressive men with neck tattoos) are safely tucked up at work. Which is interesting. His wife, although not a fellow petrol-head, understands how important this hobby is for her beloved, so when he did have a crash recently, was the first one to tell him to get back on the track and take that near-fatal corner again and again until he wasn't scared any more, despite her own fears for his safety. What a woman. Or maybe she just wanted him to die.

Although I could live without hearing another amateur runner bang on about their sad breakfast gruel and barefoot shoes, I do love hearing top athletes talk about their wives and kids, because the interaction between the track, crag or trail and the homestead is so emotional and fascinating. When he's interviewed after a race, lying half dead in his ice bath, your super-human vegan endurance runner will always thank his wife profusely for standing by him throughout his year of eating six tofu burritos at five a.m. and flying off all round the world to train at places that are a bit higher up than home. He might shed a few loving tears over the presence of his kids at the finish line, if he's not too addled by exhaustion to recognise his own kin, and that emotion is real. But it's obvious these guys put their sport first and I love watching them attempt to pretend they don't. Poor fellows – it isn't really a choice to live that way. They have to. Even amateurs will fly off to another continent in the middle of the Easter holidays to do desert marathons or Tough Mudders. They have to do it to stay feeling OK – feeling like the right kind of man – or they'd end up being even more negligent towards their families.

I am told that one of the fastest-growing sectors of the endurance sport world is the corporate event, where lawyers, financiers and other high rollers all run and swim against each other. Events like the JPMorgan Corporate Challenge pit stressed-out, over-stuffed banker against stressed-out, over-stuffed banker. Oh dear, I do hope they don't all die!

Now, I don't know if taking hallucinogens in the jungle exactly counts as a sport (although I think it does, because: sweat, commitment and feeling sick), but a friend of mine was thrown into such existential crisis by the birth of his first child that he jetted off to South America to do a week-long ayahuasca ceremony, leaving his (incensed? confused? grateful? probably all three) wife at home with the newborn. Luckily that all ended well because he came home having had a powerful vision that they ought to redecorate their house, which they did.

Of course, some of the best extreme athletes are not husbands at all, because they're not men, but adventuresome men have a lot to learn from them. Many are great writers and totally inspirational bad-asses too, like the great American rock climber Beth Rodden, who recently spoke publicly about fear:

'I get scared all the time and have cried almost every time I've been on El Cap. Growing up over twenty years ago in the climbing world it was seen as weak to admit this. But as I grew up I started to be inspired by those who didn't just "conquer" the mountain, but by those who shared their whole selves. Fear and sadness are normal and healthy and I think it's brave to show it.'*

That's quite a big thing for a top athlete to admit. And at that level (the 'multi-day, risky climbs in terrible weather' level), there's no difference between what the women and the men do. They're all hardcore nutters. So it's safe to assume that the men feel scared too (apart from the famously relaxed king of ropeless climbing, Alex Honnold who, when tested by neurologists, didn't really register fear like ordinary folk). But the point is, fear and pain are part of life for people who do extreme sports, but feeling bad doesn't put them off. In fact, like my swimmy, runny neighbour says, it attracts them. How often have you heard a blood-spattered man yell, 'Crank the gnar!' (OK, probably never) or 'hardcore' or (my personal favourite, coined by Alex Honnold when suffering ruinous altitude sickness), 'I felt a bit rugged'?†

* https://www.facebook.com/bethroddenclimb/photos/this-is-such
-a-great-reminder-for-all-of-us-but-especially-for-those-of-us-
who-a/18017309999905431/
† https://www.facebook.com/AlexHonnold/photos/just-had-my-
first-date-with-the-diamond-after-over-20-years-of-climbing-i-finall
/1704501409604154/

It's all about experiencing your body and mind as an animal. It's the opposite of Pret and the John Lewis wish list. It's a chance to get away from all the nappies and the fact that you will never move to Colorado and if you did it'd just turn out to be boring and have worse coffee and stupider people than you expected. And that is why husbands jump into rivers.

The Husband of a Certain Age: Sheds, Travel, Golf and Unexpected Passions

'A kind of second childhood falls on so many men. They trade their violence for the promise of a small increase in life span. In effect, the head of the house becomes the youngest child. And I have searched myself for this possibility with a kind of horror. For I have always lived violently, drunk hugely, eaten too much or not at all, slept around the clock or missed two nights of sleeping, worked too hard and too long in glory, or slobbed for a time in utter laziness ... My wife married a man; I saw no reason why she should inherit a baby.'

John Steinbeck, *Travels with Charley*

'The best way to get most husbands to do something is to suggest that perhaps they're too old to do it.'

Anne Bancroft

No man wants to hear it, but the similarities between old men and babies are there for all to see ('babies who look like old men' is in fact an even more popular internet search than the classic 'men who look like old lesbians'). It's not only the disrupted nights, bald heads, dodgy waterworks, toothless grins and inability to walk and have coherent views about immigration that demonstrate this cruel parallel, but the role both play in society: supposedly revered and cherished but in reality often the cause of more familial disputes and rows about money than weddings and Christmas combined. It's a wonder the divorce rates of the over-eighties are so low. Remember that joke about the old couple who went their separate ways in their nineties? 'We wanted to wait until the children were dead.'

There's no use sugar-coating it because we all know the truth: the husband over seventy is typically a cantankerous old git. He complains about his wife's strict handling of him, gripes about how she stole the best years of his life and openly teases her about whatever old lady schtick she's currently obsessed with (usually royal babies, Paul Hollywood and making her own revolting yoghurt). He flirts with nurses and makes off-colour jokes about 'Dolly Parton's lung capacity' that he'd never have done as a younger man. He will raise his eyebrows to all present when his old ball 'n' chain doesn't let him have another whisky, start arguments about 'women's lib' and switch off his hearing aid when people start talking about diet and exercise.

In the most extreme cases, inspired no doubt by Mr Twit and Chaucer and the *Carry On* films, he will play mean tricks on his wife, making her bend over for no reason or inviting her to come closer and see if there isn't something stuck in his beard.

She in turn will tell him off for making a mess with his breakfast crumbs or blood from shaving, insist he get up and fetch things for himself rather than rely on her, and point out to anyone who will listen that she could have left him in 1960 when Richard Burton asked her to hold his umbrella outside the Savoy.

All this rudeness and regret is of course a secret language that only the long married know: it's the language of a love so deep and still that the prospect of it ending is too much to bear. Baiting each other is a coping mechanism, a bit like doing something mundane in a scary situation: it fools you into thinking everything must be normal.

It also reveals the ease with which a husband can sink into a second babyhood and rather enjoy mummy wiping his chin after breakfast and telling him what's good for him. No man will admit it, and the helplessness of extreme old age is of course humiliating and horrible once the real end-game of invalidity takes hold, but after a lifetime of having to man up and take responsibility for others, many a retired gent seems to secretly thrill to the performance of being a naughty little boy again.

I had a great-uncle like this. He and his wife would come to visit and fill the house with vituperative back-and-forths like Punch and Judy. She would accuse him of being fat: he'd volley back that she looked like an ill child. She would tell him to get out from under her feet: he'd say chance would be a fine thing. He would yell at her in the car for taking a stupid route: she'd pull over and threaten to put him out on the kerb. And on and on. I came to understand that this was all by way of saying 'I love you' when we had all been out for a pub lunch one day. Great-Uncle had got outside of a sizeable portion of gammon and chips washed down with several pints of real ale, probably followed by a spotted dick and custard (because it was a long time ago now and that was a common, non-ironic thing for a pub to serve), and was looking pretty pleased with himself. We were all talking about cooking (the only safe subject in a family riven by ideological disconnects – even gardening can lead to accusations of racism when you bring invasive foreign species into it) and I asked what they'd be having for supper that night. 'Oh, I'll only be allowed an egg after this,' said Great-Unc, smiling sheepishly. His wife of sixty years shot him an almost flirty little grin that spoke of decades of even more than just love: of friendship, tolerance and, as Gwyneth Paltrow reported her parents as saying when she asked how they'd stayed together for so long, 'never both wanting to get divorced at the same time'.

Which is no mean feat, since the challenges of ageing are drastically different for women and men and can easily drive a wedge between the sexes. Women have the hormonal shock of the menopause and the realisation that no stranger will ever look at them again and say, 'I'd tap that' (which is no bad thing . . . mostly); however, for men the decline in sexual and social power is more subtle. If the midlife crisis with its new cars and embarrassing flirtations is avoided (the best words on which are attributed to Prince Philip: 'When a man opens a car door for his wife it's either a new car or a new wife'), a chap then has to decide what to do with his retirement. The concept of leisure, a cruel myth for anyone under sixty, however much he might pretend to be having fun in the twenty minutes a week when he's not working or raising children, becomes a full-time job for the husband of leisure. Especially as he will want to keep out of his wife's way as much as possible, for both their sakes.

Some develop unusual new hobbies. One man I know became obsessed with football overnight after stopping work, which was shocking to his wife as he had shown no interest in any sport whatsoever for the previous sixty years of his life. For a while she wondered what other surprising pursuits he might suddenly get into: Throat singing? Competitive eating? Thankfully, the football stuck.

Others abruptly start writing: novels, letters to *The Times*, mad blog posts, snooty TripAdvisor reviews. Clearly they have a whole lot to say and no one to listen to them, now that they can't hold forth in meetings and scribble pointless memos all day. For others, retirement is a time finally to get stuck into the alcohol and drug abuse they nobly staved off while raising children. Or perhaps a new world of yoga, meditation and CrossFit beckons? Although one wonders whether that's just a legitimate excuse to find out what wearing tights feels like. Whatever use a retiree makes of his new free time, there's no doubt that realising your wrinkled, dry-but-damp self looks like a rare ingredient that comes in a jar and goes into an Ottolenghi recipe, and that your kids think you're a moron, does something to a man. It makes him want something new. Not necessarily a new woman, but quite possibly a Wendy house in the garden. Enter the shed. Most married men do, at some point.

For thousands of years, a blasted heath or boggy bit of moorland would do, if there was a shepherd's hut or spreading chestnut tree under which to get some peace. Coleridge's 'This Lime-Tree Bower My Prison'? He loved it! Didn't want to go on that walk at all. Even Stone Age man must have retreated to a dark corner of the main dwelling when he needed some time away from the wife, and I've always known in my heart that the decorated caves of Lascaux were no more than proto-sheds where grizzled old dudes in animal skins could express them-selves doodling pointless little stick men and creating a pub-like environment with a few dry snacks and a nice damp floor.

These days, sheds are eliding with the trendy 'tiny homes' movement and being marketed to men as cool retreats. The Shed of the Year contest is over a decade old and its 'Readers' Sheds' web page ('the home of the Great British Shed in all its forms') shows some truly awesome and many rather alarming attempts at

Englishmen making their sheds their castles. A few are made by and for women, but most have names like 'The Sir Hugo Dreadnought' (yes, naming your shed is important) and contain a lot of beer mats. These are man caves. The decidedly Readers' Wives quality of the photography adds to the forbidden feeling of voyeurism as we peep into sheds containing collections of Lego, left-handed guitars and magician's equipment. [*]

   The UK firm Waltons Garden Buildings has a section of its e-shop called 'man caves', advertising Wendy houses for 'gents', as they call their punters, offering to 'Create a space of your own for watching sport, playing bar games or just having a little snooze'.[†] Looking at the pictures of these summer-house-style sheds, with their cute gabling and tiny verandas, I recognise them as identical to the kids' playhouses I was checking out for my daughter the other day. Only they're not painted pale pink, and are festooned with blokey ephemera: lawn mowers suggestively poking out of the doorway; a big gas barbecue straddling the veranda. Now, I well understand the appeal of a Wendy house, so I can tell you the meaning of these manly playhouses: they are a place to live your life without the boss of your real house – shall we call her mummy? – telling you off. You can eat and drink naughty things at funny times of day (Iced Gems for breakfast! Hurrah!), invite only your chosen friends

---

[*] http://www.readersheds.co.uk/share.cfm?SHARESHED=6281
[†] https://www.waltons.co.uk/man-caves

to come in (no boys/girls/grownups allowed) and leave it as messy as you like. Heck, you can get into a sleeping bag, ram a plank of wood across your lap and write violent children's stories all day while eating chocolate biscuits, like Roald Dahl did, a man whose unpleasant experience of authority in the form of boarding school, the army and hospitals made him quite naturally gravitate towards a little wooden kingdom of his own. And wasn't John Steinbeck's motorhome Rocinante just a shed on wheels? We learn in *Travels With Charley* that he stocked it up with booze, weapons and a dog (albeit a giant fluffy poodle; but then again Dirty Den had one of those and so does Chris Packham and they are both All Man, as every 1980s telly addict knows) and travelled away from his wife in it.

Of course, there's one thing a man can't easily do in a shed, and that's chuck balls around, which brings us to that mainstay of the over-fifties Western male, golf. Golf. Why? A colleague of mine, who freely indulges in the apparently feminine sport of extreme gossip sessions, and with whom I often talk about how potty it is that society has gendered even talking to appear 'sissy' when done a certain way, described going on an experimental golfing trip with some straight old men one day in the name of research. He was intrigued to discover what they would talk about over several hours walking around the course with no women around. Surely they'd get stuck into some end-of-the-pier anecdotes about ladies' big bottoms or that time they did mushrooms at university and tried to have sex with a molehill? No they did not. The talk remained so small and superficial that my mate compared it to what you might say if you're trying to talk someone down from a panic attack: 'Oh look at that squirrel! Lovely breeze! We'll have a nice cup of tea later!' For hours and hours.

It's not that men are incapable of gossip. My colleague says that his female friends' husbands seem to relish him coming round for dinner so they can legitimately get stuck into some cheeky chatter and speculation about other people's marriages or family ructions or even something really outrageous and gay like clothing and food. Imagine! But it's just not seemly to talk like this when alone with other straight men.

I asked a keen golfer friend, Sol, to keep an ear out for the chat amongst his golfing buddies next time they met up at the club. Here is his shocking report:

'Today I played eighteen holes of intense competitive golf on a stunningly beautiful morning with three other married men. I paid attention to the conversation. Ninety per cent was about yardage, wind conditions, speed of the greens, and condition of the fairways. The other 10 per cent was football, politics, winter holidays. And these were professional, educated, emotionally intelligent men.'

Now, my secret spy on the golf course is not, I think it's fair to say, an Englishman. And he, like others who fate decreed to be born in places better and worse than this sceptred isle, reckons all this reticence is just classic

English repression. But I've watched Frenchmen play pétanque, Greeks play *tavli*, and Americans play poker, and I get the same vibe from each group. It's all about the game. And yes, the game might sometimes be working as a dynamic metaphor for their deepest feelings (betrayal round the poker table; bad luck on the backgammon board; desire to stop for a pastis on the boules alley), but they are definitely not gossiping about their wives while waiting for their turn. They are laser-focused on their play. And while we must whenever possible resist saying things are 'genetically hard-wired' into us, because the science of nature vs. nurture in gender is still embryonic, it's impossible to ignore that – for whatever reason – men love and are brilliant at not getting distracted from a task that involves rules and has a beginning and an end. There's probably an excellent psychological term for it but I bet it isn't exciting and manly enough, so let's call it the one-track lockdown game-state. And the one-track lockdown game-state does not get sidetracked by loose chat. End of.

There does exist the occasional husband-at-rest who, like a chilled teenager, likes to do not much at all with his autumn years. And doing nothing with one's wife can be an indicator of a happy and long marriage, as one veteran of matrimony told me when I asked him the secret of his happy set-up:

'It helps to enjoy just being together and doing nothing much. With some couples I think they need the company of others or an activity to do together to keep the relationship going.' Although there is one mutually interesting activity that this same fellow credits with playing an important part in maintaining wedded bliss:

'Sex. Without a strong physical attraction and a wish to share a bed each night, I can't see how a full and happy relationship can survive a lifetime together. It always puzzles me when I read about physical attraction lessening significantly after the first few years together . . . there doesn't have to be rampant sex every night, but it does help if touching and cuddling remains something both partners want and need.'

And in case you're imagining this particular interviewee is one of those soppy fellows who leaps about with roses between his teeth, let me assure you that he is as hard and rational as an abacus, as proven by his take on the meaning of love and the fact that he wears shoes at breakfast:

'I am sceptical about the words "being in love with". I think "need" and "being dependent on" more accurately define my feelings for my wife. There is a long list of things which my wife contributes to my life, and in which she scores 9, 10 or 11 out of 10 . . . and very few where her score is down at 1, 2 or 3. If it were the other way round, I doubt if I would be saying that I am still in love with her after nearly forty years together.'

The majority of older husbands I spoke to would never be so candid with me, yet I'm eternally fascinated by their take on lifelong love, so take my chances with anyone I meet who seems as if they might want to talk, or be drunk.

The other day I got to combine both of these, as I bumped into a family friend in his mid-seventies while travelling. A candid sort, and both of us verbally lubricated by the fraternity and claustrophobia of air travel (and of sitting side by side instead of facing each other – why don't more therapists try this arrangement?), he told me how things were in his long marriage. Turns out they're pretty good! They were bad for a while, and then their kids grew up and they could have separated but they decided they liked each other too much. Now they have a different sort of marriage that sounds like a wonderful friendship. I didn't ask about their sex life as that's a sure-fire way to make someone clam up, but he did say that having slept next to the same woman for over thirty years, he has noticed her body gradually changing as he sees and touches 'her ageing skin'. He finds it – he looks for the right word – 'moving'. He didn't smile or frown when he said this but I felt that it was spoken in the awareness of mortality skulking round a not-too-distant corner. And of a great love.

A lifelong marriage, with its slow changes and revolutions, is pure poetry. The pulling apart and re-forming; the slow march, hand in hand, or not, towards the inevitable end. It's amazing to see. I am privileged to know quite a few pretty aged married couples and I guess it's the Mediterranean diet because many of them are Greek. Or English with houses on the Greek island where I spend my holidays, who I suppose must have ingested enough fresh fish and olive oil to still both be kicking in their seventies and eighties. And while all older couples delight and inspire me in some way, I can't help noticing the differences between the way northern and southern Europeans behave in their autumn years . . .

As we fly out to Greece each spring and summer, I can spot the Englishmen even before the EasyJet check-in because of their predictable linen uniform and the look on their faces: surprisingly scowly considering they don't have to go to work and never fought in the war. Perhaps it's just the indignity of flying on a budget airline (the quickest way to get to the island for most of the year)? After all, these guys are old enough to recall the golden age of air travel, so must resent not being passed a glass of champagne and greeted by name when they board the plane. They certainly all seem to get highly exercised about Speedy Boarding and overhead locker space and delays.

Although many of these post-breeding pairs are in fine shape and nicely accessorised with good sunglasses and financial freedom, they are not to be found canoodling and giggling like the skittish empty-nester I propose to be when I'm old and thin and brown. Because rather than spending their retirement pootling down a canal drinking wine like national treasures and icons of how to age cheerfully Timothy West and Prunella Scales, they've saddled themselves with the pain of a second home (or at least an endless whirl of tiring foreign jaunts). So they just bicker about insurance and car hire and whose fault it is that their adult children don't want to join them.

I gaze at these fine-looking but anxious gentlefolk, the husbands especially, and I can't help thinking what stops them being happy is a terrible insecurity about what sort of Englishman abroad they want to be. You see, this island we go to, let's call it Corfu, is divided strictly across the middle. The top end is full of posh people, rich people, fake posh people and ordinary middle-class families splurging on a villa holiday. The other end is a raucous Bacchanal of cheap nightclubs, English pubs, greasy spoons and ... well, I don't know what else because obviously I've never been there, our base being conveniently located slap bang in the middle of the island, away from both factions. Anyway, up front in the plane – in those seats you can pay a few quid extra to occupy – are always several rows of silver-haired retired couples, or sometimes chaps on their own, flying out to join their wives or oversee a bit of building work on their holiday homes, and they all look exactly like this:

Linen trousers in white, cream or blue; a pink or blue shirt either in heavy washed linen or light cotton; loafers; a panama hat; iPhone in a leather case in their breast pocket; a summery but not seersucker sports jacket; a large handkerchief sticking out of their jacket pocket and a copy of *The Times*. I know they want to be reading the *Mail*, as some of the bolder wives do (because women give up on what people think of them sooner than men do – we reach saturation point after forty years of being on the receiving end of the world's judgy gaze), but they daren't be seen with it because that would be seriously off-brand. The fake posh of the Ionian have to carry so much symbolism in their every seam, turn-up and hatband that it's no wonder they look stressed.

Get in amongst them, as I have done for the last fifteen years, and you'll find a few renegades. Last year I met a man who, instead of all the flouncy linen, was wearing a sort of fisherman's utility waistcoat. On his head was not a panama or Borsalino (which is what truly fancy types wear, but you rarely see them because they tend to fly private or arrive by yacht), but a white cotton bucket-hat like little boys wear. He was old and interesting-looking, and had some intriguing kit hanging out of his many pockets: a few feathers; a small notebook; a bit of bread wrapped in foil (the linen crew don't eat or drink anything on the plane in case it looks common). He looked like a man fully kitted out to make the most of his retirement. I struck up a conversation with him. It turned out he was a great lover of wildlife, particularly birds, and on retiring from work had chosen to live out most of each year in the fragrant hills of the Mediterranean, immersed in nature. We had a long, cheery chat about buzzards, and his tanned face broke into a joyous smile over and over again. Wife? Children? Nineteen-year-old Gypsy lover? All of the above, probably. This was one happy old dude because he knew what he loved and was getting after it like a pro. He was free. His presence was a balm to me and reminded me we needn't fear getting old.

So much for the ageing Brits. Want to know how Greek husbands do it? Awesomely, of course, and key to this is how they gear married life towards maintaining self-respect and ensuring a constant supply of good food and company. Your classic septuagenarian Hellene is shored up against death by means of an impressive arsenal: first, his moustache, which is thick and well tended, whether it be white or black. Next, his English-style tailoring, which looks far better than real English clothes because it's made by an Italian. He keeps fit by swimming in the sea every morning, and happy by gossiping loudly and railing against the government with a big, angry grin on his face. He eats lovely food, of course, by which I mean food that makes him happy, and does so by the light of the moon. He has a doctor who knows that while peppermint tea is very bad for a sensitive digestion, coffee and fags are fine. He falls in love, does business deals, and drinks moderately until the day he dies. He sometimes gets bashed on the side of the head by his screeching wife as she's riding pillion on his motor scooter, but that's a small price to pay for all the life-giving *spanakopita* and sweet, gritty coffee she makes him.

Stroll the bougainvillaea-strewn backstreets of a Corfiot town at nightfall and you'll see groups of women in their sixties, seventies, eighties, nineties, and that special Greek age where you look like a walnut, wear black and have four dyed black hairs pulled across your pate. They are sitting together, with a jumble of toddlers, dogs and cats at their feet, and they are having a right laugh and not planning to go inside any time soon. Their husbands? They're down the road outside the *kafeneion* doing what they like best too: watching the telly with the sound down through the open door of the bar, smoking, grumbling and lecturing each other and any passing youngsters about sex, football and politics.

The men and women are not together all the time. Of course they're not. They want different things. Their happy segregation makes the long evenings of retirement a much more collegiate place for married folk. And by not keeping to themselves and staying in watching *Bargain Hunt*, as their English equivalents might be, they have a far stronger support structure if and when they find themselves coping alone. Which, as we shall see in the next chapter, is the final hurdle in the Husband's Progress.

The Recidivist Husband

'Marriage is the triumph of imagination over intelligence. Second marriage is the triumph of hope over experience.'

Oscar Wilde

In 'Husbands Alone', we learned about what men do when their wives are out. Many of those I interviewed positively lit up when they spoke of their one-on-zero time. Which is not to say they don't adore their other halves, it's just that there are things men like doing that really annoy women. Smelly things. Loud things. Stupid things. Of course there's a lot that wives do that drive their partners crazy too, as we've heard: everything from giving more affection to the family pet than to the man of the house, to obsessive tidying. So yes, we all need time to ourselves, and we'll probably never honestly admit to anybody all the weird stuff we get up to when no one's around.

But anyone who has reached the age where divorce and widowhood have begun to cast a shadow over their social group will notice a crucial difference between men and women. When it comes to really being alone – when a partner is gone and not coming back – men will get back on the marital horse like a rat up a drain. Which is actually a perfect mixed metaphor for how confused and animalistic our responses to loss are.

Statistics back this up, but it's such an accepted feature of life that we all know it to be true.* A widower will waste no time at all in filling that wife-shaped space, whereas a woman left alone will take much longer to even consider a new intimate friendship, let alone a marriage.

There are a few hypotheses for why this happens. The traditional view is that men can't take care of themselves, and after a few months of burnt toast and crusty towels they cut their losses and find a woman – any woman – to look after them. That may have been true in the past, and was definitely a consideration when so many women died in childbirth and left working men with a brood of young to raise. But these days most husbands are quite able to cook and clean (and, who knows, may be rather excellent at it away from the critical eyes of the Head of Domestic Services).

Pertinent to this was the chat I had with a wife of our parish the other day. One of those surprisingly moving conversations that start out about the rubbish collection and end up with a misty eye or two. This lady, in her sixties

---

* https://www.goldbergjones-sandiego.com/divorce/remarriage-statistics/

I reckon, said she forces her reluctant husband to get involved with cooking and cleaning because one day she might not be around, and it 'wouldn't be loving' to leave him helpless. He's quite a good cook now, apparently.

So there may be something else at play, aside from the fact that in our messed-up society, a saggy sixty-year-old man with a house is considered more sexually attractive than his female counterpart. Could it be that a man suddenly bereft morphs into an irresistibly attractive love-god and women just can't leave him alone? I wonder. On the face of it, a man who cries a lot and sits in a dirty house surrounded by old photographs is not what every woman wants. But I can imagine getting to know a bereaved man; maybe helping him sort his house out a bit and giving him a good meal. How lovely it would be to see the happy transformation your work has effected: blotchy cheeks and sad eyes start to glow and sparkle; the first real smile; he starts wanting to be more active and take an interest in the world (and you). Hmm. Doesn't it sound like raising a baby? Mightn't it give a woman the same exhilarated rush of wonder at the way a human can grow and develop? Wouldn't it be a bit of a power trip? So yes, I bet a newly lonely man could be quite an enticing project for a woman who doesn't have a newborn or rescue cat to hand. And, since the absent first wife is either gone for ever or, in the case of an acrimonious divorce, public enemy number one, the new one can agree wholeheartedly when he recalls what an angel or a bitch she was.

There's an excellent theory about men's enthusiasm for remarriage, based on the notion that men are primed (whether by genes, culture or both) to find the world a generally hostile place that needs to be fought and overcome.* The poor soldiers go through life with pistols cocked, ready to attack one of the many threats to their wellbeing, family, home and very manhood that lurk around every corner. Women, the theory goes, are a bit more chilled out and accepting of the slings and arrows of fortune, plus they have awesome collaborative ways of dealing with trouble and pain alongside their sisters. But the man is a lone warrior and, as I've discovered in my interviews with husbands, even the home can be a battleground. Home as a place of danger? That's a tricky idea for a domestically inclined woman like me to get her head around, but I've heard it over and over again: home, for a husband, is a place where you can feel much worse than in the outside world.

It's a place where he can fail at strange jobs that he didn't know he was supposed to be good at, like folding towels properly. It's a place where lost intimacy and affection might follow him around like a ghost. A place that costs him money he doesn't have. Essentially, it's often someone else's place – his wife's domain.

So when the man of the house finds himself home alone for ever, he naturally feels very scared. 'He avoids

* https://www.nytimes.com/2012/01/08/fashion/why-men-cant-stand-to-be-alone-after-a-breakup-or-a-divorce.html

danger, aware that only so many arrows are granted to him in a lifetime, so he should husband his resources. Being alone feels dangerous to a man,' writes Dominique Browning of this phenomenon in *The New York Times*.*

I am convinced that this theory – combined with a bit of good old Freudian mummy trouble – is what drives bereaved men to remarry in such high numbers.

The deeper truth hidden in these statistics and inter-pretations is that marriage represents something deeply sweet and proper which men, those romantic, fearful old souls, never give up on. Being a husband rather than a boyfriend (or companion or late-flowering lover – has anyone yet found a good word for an eighty-year-old male partner? Gerontoflame, perhaps?) feels good, because calling yourself a husband cushions your iden-tity against the barbs of lonely, unloved old age. It sounds like you're a man who can still care and provide for someone. And that somebody chose you. That someone wants you to bring them coffee in the morning (and hope and poetry). It's a bold anti-death move, especially when made in the face of death itself.

It takes an honest man to say 'I'm old and alone and I need this' and to say it in public, with a ring and a pub reception for twenty with sandwiches and your grown-up children looking on with a mixture of relief and anxi-ety about their inheritance. And an honest man, at the end of life, is a happy man.

* Ibid.

Conclusion

Men marry for love, security and status. Just like women. Men want to be left alone sometimes to do stuff that seems silly when someone else is looking. Just like women. Thousands of years of brutal, short human lives, through which babies had to be made and fed, and enemies repelled, made men learn to act like warriors and women less so. Those years grew a strong and useful patriarchy, but now things are changing. The dangers that face us today are more abstract, and we can easily ignore them for a long time while we live cocooned in cities. However, the feeling that he is expected to be a warrior still burns inside every man. For some, it's a horrible expectation that he can barely acknowledge. Others rather like it. Which is why for every married man who runs away from his wife each Saturday to fling himself at a mountainside or run until he can't breathe, there's one who holes up with his cats and books and gets his kicks in a gentler way. The secret lives of husbands are as diverse, surprising, reassuring, silly, sexy and alarming as the human race itself.

For us spouses, this represents a challenge. How can we be respectful of their mysterious ways and not try to change them, when sometimes what they do seems bafflingly insane, stupid or harmful? Perhaps simply by listening to them and encouraging them to talk. And knowing that sometimes – often – they need to be left alone. Give them space to breathe and they'll use that breath to say nice things to you when they come back.

Preparing this book, I found it much easier than I expected just to sit and let men talk. Sometimes they wriggled and writhed and made jokes and apologised for being boring and checked their phones a lot – behaviours I know well because I do them too. But if I just kept sitting there, 'calm-assertive', as César Millán, the Mexican Dog Whisperer says, when dealing with an anxious dachshund, and tried not to interrupt too much, most interviewees opened up beyond both of our expectations. We learned a lot. Unexpected things were said.

Listening is a pleasure and a gift. Let's all do it a bit more, and see what riches it might bring to ourselves, our husbands, our families and our world.

Also, they really like telly and blow jobs.

Acknowledgements

Thanks to the colleagues, friends and fellow travellers who have helped me while working on this book: Lindsey Anderson, Tuesday Benfield, Richard Beswick, Benet Catty, Claire Chesser, Giles Coren, Amanda Craig, Christine Davis, Ant Harwood, Mr and Mrs Ivan Helmer, Penelope Isaac, Carola Long, Marily Macvicar, Robbie Millen, Justin Myers, Rebecca Rose, Jordan Scott, Mr and Mrs Jamie Stevenson, Erica Wagner, Esther Walker, Robert Weiss, Beth Wright.

Many thanks to Toby Helm for his kind permission to quote from his article, 'World War I memories: my grandfather's story', which appeared in *The Guardian* on 3 November 2013 and is still available online, and to Rogers, Coleridge & White Literary Agency for permission to reference Edward St Aubyn's thoughts on fatherhood, detailed in 'Inheritance' by Ian Parker, which appeared in the *New Yorker* on 2 June 2014.

Special thanks to all the awesome men who let me interrogate them for this book. I understand why you want to remain anonymous, but I wish I could put your names in lights in recognition of the honesty and generosity you showed me as I poked around in your brains like a dumb tourist.

Extra special thanks to Peter, Alec and Marily. I love you, fam.